W9-BVW-176

BUT YOU KNEW
THAT ALREADY

BUT YOU KNEW
THAT ALREADY

WHAT A PSYCHIC CAN
TEACH YOU ABOUT LIFE

DOUGALL FRASER

RODALE

Printed in the United States of America
Rodale Inc. makes every effort to use acid-free ∞, recycled paper ♲ .

Book design by Christina Gaugler

Library of Congress Cataloging-in-Publication Data

Fraser, Dougall.
     But you knew that already : what a psychic can teach you about life / Dougall Fraser.
           p.   cm.
     ISBN-13 978–1–59486–136–9 hardcover
     ISBN-10 1–59486–136–6 hardcover
     1. Fraser, Dougall.   2. Psychics—United States—Biography.   I. Title.
BF1027.F73A3   2005
133.8'092—dc22   2004028079

Distributed to the book trade by Holtzbrinck Publishers
2 4 6 8 10 9 7 5 3 1 hardcover

For David, for everything

Contents

Acknowledgments

THERE ARE SO MANY PEOPLE THAT WERE A PART OF MAKING THIS BOOK POSSIBLE. I'd like to start by thanking my family: David, Mom, Dad, Tarrin, and Bill. Your support in my life has made it possible for me to make my dreams come true.

It has taken a while for me to find the right team for this project, but many people have been involved in and supportive of seeing this book find the right home: Kimyla Guice-Stegall, Meredith Kaufman, Anthony Flacco, Chad Ryan (for the title), Linda Konner, Marilyn Kentz, Nancy Alspaugh, Sandi with Americall, and Donna LeBlanc.

To my editor, Mariska van Aalst, thank you for seeing my vision. You have been supportive of the entire process, and I am grateful for the chance. The entire staff at Rodale has made me feel welcome, honored, and appreciated, and I thank all of you.

To my agent, Sharlene Martin, your tenacity for this project is by far one of the greatest gifts I have ever received. You are not only a wonderful agent but, more importantly, a dear friend.

I did not write this book alone. Julie McCarron has worked for hours with me on this project. I have learned so much during this process. Julie, thank you for helping me make sense. For taking the clutter of my words and gently teaching me how to make them flow. Your talent is very, very large, and I know that your future will be filled with great success!

And finally, I would like to thank all of my spiritual teachers: Dixie Richards, Terrie Kolb, Dr. Jeffrey Chernin, Carolyn Solis, Angela Lusk, APLE foundation, and all of my clients—your lessons are my lessons.

Introduction

I CANNOT READ YOUR MIND. Truth be told, even if I could, I'm not sure I would want to. As a professional psychic and clairvoyant, I have the ability to see your strengths and weaknesses. When I am centered, I am able to perceive your hopes and dreams. More importantly, I can guide you in making them happen. I can tell you a physical description of the love of your life, but sadly I can't see his or her phone number.

I have worked in the New Age community for more than 10 years. I have done readings at psychic fairs and UFO conventions. In the past 10 years, I have read for every kind of person, from janitors to A-list celebrities. I've worked for several of the most prominent psychic hotlines. I have seen the good, the bad, and the ugly sides of the psychic community. And now I am ready to tell you all about it.

Know this as my truth: I love my work. However, I am perfectly comfortable laughing at the fact that I am a professional psychic. Think about it: I'm a modern-day fortune-teller. And I adore it. In this day and age, just like every past day and age, people are fascinated by psychic phenomena. Whether it's an infomercial at 3 A.M. with a Jamaican woman wrapped in her green headdress, promising you love and fortune for the low fee of $5 a minute, or a television talk show where audience members are connected with their dear departed loved ones, the come-ons are everywhere.

My experience has been quite different, and I'd like to share my journey with you. (I'll change the names of all my clients to protect their privacy, something I feel very strongly about.)

Here's the thing: I do not talk to the dead; think of me as the psychic who talks to the living. I have been given the ability to instantly perceive many of your personal characteristics and desires—both positive and negative—just from the sound of your voice. But I did not inherit this ability from my grandmother; I was not born on a day of perfect planetary alignment. I have struggled to accept my gifts and find my voice, and I think it is important to show you that process: the times I have been right, yes, but also the times I have been wrong. My job is certainly unique, but my ability is more common than you might think. This is my story.

Chapter One

JUST YOUR AVERAGE DAY

BEFORE MY 3 O'CLOCK CLIENT ARRIVES, I focus on her name and uncomfortably realize that I have only recently read for her. I'm more than happy to help people when I can, but I try to stick to a rule: Clients are only allowed to book one psychic reading a year with me. But because I no longer do my own booking—a fact that has released me from years of being chained to my phone—this rule has become a bit harder to enforce. One reading a year is plenty. (Okay, so maybe if you are having a year like Martha Stewart, you could get two.)

I remember Joanne before I go out to retrieve her in the reception area. As we say hello, my heart feels heavy, but I want to do something—how can I help her? She settles herself in the comfortable wing chair in my office, and I close my eyes to begin our work. As always, I say a quick prayer, asking that only energy of the highest good enter my being.

"Joanne, why are you here again?" I ask. She looks taken aback by the question. "Nothing has really changed since our last session together. You are still with your husband, though we both know that this relationship has failed. You don't want to live in your home. When you suggest to your husband that your life and relationship could and should be better, he laughs at you."

"I know," she sobs. "*You* know," she adds in hushed awe. (That awe stuff always embarrasses me. People, it's what I do.)

Like many clients, Joanne is here in the hopes of eliciting the response she wants to hear from me. She wants me to tell her that in a few months her husband will fall back in love with her, that he will get a new job, and that her life will be magically transformed.

I see none of that happening, and I can't lie to her.

"I've been to an astrologer who told me we would stay together," she tells me, anxiously searching my eyes. I don't respond but ask myself: *How can I help her?* "A tarot reader said he was cheating on me," she offers, clearly eager to hear me contradict that assertion. I don't. "I'm seeing my therapist twice a week," she says. Still not speaking, I concentrate harder: *How can I help her?* "I'm trying a new herbal medicine for depression. This one is supposed to work—really."

Joanne is spending probably hundreds of dollars every month in the desperate hope that someone will give her a remedy, a quick cure—one that does not exist. I feel her desperation. Over and over I whisper in my mind: *How can I help her?*

Only Wellbutrin will help her, another voice whispers in my mind.

"A numerologist thought I was single," she says. "What does that mean?"

"Joanne," I begin, "I see you are a graceful, persistent, and courageous woman. You've lost touch with that woman. We need to find her for you again. You are giving your power away—to me, other advisors, your boss, and most of all, your husband.

"Joanne, you have to find your voice. You have to ask yourself, in every area of your life, *What motivates me? What kind of existence do I want?* I see your potential, but there is always free will. At the moment, your current life trend is going to continue to keep you in a state of depression. The next time you want a reading, I want you to take that money and invest it in you."

I finish her session by saying the same thing I always do: "We have covered all of your issues, Joanne. Now it's your turn to change them."

Thing is, I don't want my clients to look to me as a spiritual superman with the power to give all the answers. Instead, I want them to relate to me as an adviser who can help them find that power within themselves. I want everyone to realize: You have your own answers, if you'll only listen. Honor the work, but don't put me on a pedestal.

Now it's just a few minutes before 4 o'clock, and I am anxious that my next client will be late. I am always punctual—in fact, I am invariably, annoyingly early—but I need to stop expecting that from everyone. I close my eyes and center myself. My mental calendar appears in my mind. It's Friday afternoon, and after my last client, I will pick up my boyfriend and head off for a weekend away. Perhaps my 4 o'clock forgot about her session and I will get to leave early!

The receptionist finally buzzes. "Dougall, Diane is here to see you." No such luck. By this time, it is 10 minutes past 4.

"Okay, I'll be right out."

As I walk to the waiting room, I try to conceal my irritation that Diane is late. Maybe she took the wrong subway, or maybe she got lost—who knows? There are a million things that could have happened. I need to stay calm. I peer through the glass door and see a new face in the waiting room. Diane is perched on the couch, talking rapidly into her cell phone. I guess that she's about 30 years old. I quickly take in her perfect manicure, her beautifully blown-out hair, her wildly expensive shoes, and her diamond jewelry. This woman is striking.

"Diane?"

"I gotta go, I gotta go." She slams her cell phone closed and stands up. "Yes, I'm Diane."

"Hi, Diane, I'm Dougall Fraser."

Diane is a woman dressed for power. She has on a crimson cashmere sweater neatly tucked into a leather skirt. As I guide her to my office, her heels click confidently on the wooden floors. Diane's head turns from side to side, looking at the walls of the corridor.

"Not what you expected?" I ask.

"Not at all."

Most people seem a little shocked that I conduct sessions in a traditional office space—no garish neon palms in the window. My clients could just as easily be visiting their accountant or nutritionist as meeting with a psychic. I make sure to have incense burning and at least one crystal on my desk to engage their fantasies as to what a psychic *should* be.

But when I first moved to this office space, I briefly entertained the idea of decorating my room as perhaps a traditional psychic might. I thought, *What would Oda Mae do?* (Oda Mae Brown, as you recall, was Whoopi Goldberg's character in the movie *Ghost.*) I would greet my clients wrapped in a gold blousy muumuu, parting the beads hanging in my doorway. I would lead them to a circular table, taking deep breaths as I prepare to contact the other side.

Thankfully, I decided to stick with Standard Office instead of Early Psychic Nut Job, and that has made all the difference.

I open the door to my private oasis. Diane sizes up the office and instinctively sits in the appropriate seat. She turns her cell phone off, lays her black leather bag to her left, looks up, and smiles. I am warmed by her beautiful smile—she really is extremely pretty.

"I am so excited to be here."

Okay, so she has completely won me over. I'm charmed—I no longer care that she arrived late.

I start by speeding through my explanation process. This is her first reading ever. A virgin, as it were.

"Diane, I am going to start with a quick prayer; then I will ask you to say your first name out loud, okay?"

"My full name?"

Truth be told, it does not matter. The reason I ask people to say their name out loud is that I need a few extra seconds to prepare to begin the session. And to be perfectly honest, I am simply awful with names.

"Just the name that you go by every day, whatever people call you."

I close my eyes and move through my prayer. With each word, my mind gets ready to shut down for the next 30 minutes. I take deep breaths and exhale fully. Slowly my body begins to tingle; there is a tangible shift in the air. With each exhale, my life leaves this room and this place as I unfold my entire consciousness to be with Diane. When I open my eyes, she is staring right back at me. Her look has changed from one of excitement to one of anxiety. Her brow is crinkled as if she were looking through me and not at me.

"Please say your name for me three times."

"Diane, Diane, Diane."

As she says her name, she becomes blanketed in pink light. I no longer see her face as the entire room is enveloped in this pink energy. It welcomes me. I breathe it in and prepare my first statement to her.

"Diane. You, my dear, are a perfectionist."

"Ha! That's an understatement!" she laughs.

Usually when I start a session, I like to loosen the person up. I generally start with a few compliments before going to the core of the issue. But Diane is different. Her body language tells me she is a no-nonsense kind of girl.

"Your perfection issues are both a blessing and a curse. In business, it has made you a success. You are in a position of power, a creative field. It feels like a dream job."

"I work in advertising."

"I see you at the vice president level or above. Is that the case?"

"I am the VP for creative affairs at my agency, yes."

"Pink light is the light of perfection. It is easy to see how your desire for perfection has aided you in your business career. More importantly, we need to explore how it holds you back as well."

"How can a good trait hold me back?"

"Good question, but I don't know yet. Let me continue. It is your destiny to work in the business world, and you certainly seem to have made your mark there. But that is where most of your energy lies, in your career."

"I love my work."

"I know you do, but you are more than your work. Your heart feels lonely, which is strange, considering you are in a relationship."

"I'm not lonely." Her tone is defensive. "I'm practically engaged."

"Diane, you are either engaged or you're not, and at this time you are, in fact, not engaged. Actually, your relationship is in jeopardy. Who is Jeff?"

"Jeff is my older brother." She starts to say more, then stops herself. Diane's brown eyes are now the size of saucers. She is leaning forward in her chair, waiting to hear what I'll say next.

I have to say, nothing pleases me more than getting a name right. I can't explain how on earth I do that. The best way to describe it is like a cosmic text message to my brain.

"Jeff has health issues, yes?"

"He is retarded. I wouldn't really call it a health issue."

"Well, I may be getting this a little muddled, but somehow your life issues relate to your brother. Bear with me for just a second. You are a professional woman in her midthirties; you have a thriving career and a handsome, terrific boyfriend. Yet you and I both know that you are tired and lonely, right?"

"I don't think of myself as lonely," she protests. "Tired, yes, of course. Who isn't?"

"By lonely, I mean that you only depend on yourself. Admirable, but exhausting as well. You are demanding far too much of yourself, setting standards for yourself that are too high, and counting only on yourself—for everything."

"I don't think setting high standards for myself is a problem. It's gotten me a long way."

"Okay. Let's go back to your childhood for a moment. You are the younger child."

"How did you know that?"

"You just told me that Jeff was your older brother," I remind her. (I don't see *everything* psychically.)

"Oh, right."

"You were the younger child. Your older brother was somewhat handicapped, and I can clearly see you had to take care of yourself from the very beginning of your life. In some ways, I think your parents expected too much from you. They expected you to be perfect; meanwhile, they were overwhelmed with the needs of your brother."

"Now you sound like my therapist."

"Diane, during high school your perfection issues were at their worst."

Diane winces in shame, and her entire body tenses. She clearly does not want me to talk about this. I am fairly certain she had an eating disorder when she was a teen, but I'm reluctant to bring it up to her. What if I'm wrong? Worse, what if I am right? How does this affect anything now? She looks perfectly healthy, and yet I can feel something pinched and hungry radiating from her core. Clearly she doesn't starve herself physically anymore, but . . . she starves herself emotionally. That's it.

"Diane, please hear me out: Did you have an eating disorder in your teenage years?"

"I can't believe you just said that. I did have anorexia for a couple of years. I wasn't hospitalized or anything, but I did have to go to therapy for a long time before I got better. I have never told this to anyone. Only my parents know."

"You have to understand that when we are created, we have strengths and weaknesses that manifest in different ways. I think because of your brother's disability, you took it upon yourself to overcompensate. You became the perfect daughter. During adolescence, it got out of hand, and you began to starve yourself because you did not feel like you deserved nourishment, literally."

Diane is now crying. This woman, who only 15 minutes ago appeared to have New York in the palm of her hand, is now just a lost, awkward teenager.

"Diane, you feel much more authentic to me now than you did when you walked through my door. Have you spoken to your boyfriend about this stuff?"

"Not really. He knows about Jeff and my struggle with that, but not about the anorexia."

"Will you do me a favor? Tonight I want you to talk to him about all of this. Blame it on me. Say that it was my idea. I think when you air all of your history, this persistent sense of loneliness will go away. Let him in. You don't have to be perfect; he will still love you. And you don't have to bear every burden alone. That's what partners are for."

"I never thought of it like that."

As I look over Diane's shoulder, I realize that we only have a few minutes left. Time to wrap things up.

"Do you have any questions, Diane?"

"Will I ever be happily married to Peter?"

"I think so. I think he is a good match for you. You just need to slow down your life. You are running around like a crazy woman, striving for perfection; meanwhile, you haven't realized that your life is already in harmony. Peter, your boss, your family—they can all see the flaws in you, yet they still adore you. My question is, when are you going to relax and adore yourself, even with a few flaws?"

"I still don't know what you mean by flaws."

I can tell it's the word "flaw" that gives her the most trouble. I think for a second: How can I put this into words she'll understand? "You don't seem to enjoy your life, and I think that much of your stress is self-created. Rather than delegate tasks to others at work, you do them yourself. You busy yourself, constantly creating long days. The job gets done, of course, but it could get done earlier. For example, why were you late today?"

"I'm sorry. I had some things to wrap up at the office, and then my mother called."

"Okay, so what did you have to wrap up at the office?"

"Well, now that I think about it, I was in front of your building on time. It was my mother's call that distracted me. I had to answer it."

"If you had let her call go to voice mail, you would have been on time, correct?"

"Correct."

"And if you had been on time, then we would not have had to rush this session, correct?"

"Correct."

"This is a perfect example. You and I both know your mom calls 18 times a day with nothing important on her mind, but in your quest to be the perfect daughter, you answer each and every time."

"I never thought of it that way."

"I'm not saying to ignore your mom, but as I scan through your life, there appear to be a number of things that pull you away from the now, whether it be your boss, your mom, your ego—any number of things, really."

She looks at me intently, with her eyebrow crinkled. "I'm confused as to what to do with all of this information."

"Okay, here is your homework: In the next month, I want you to keep a very detailed account of how you spend your day. How many hours are dedicated to work, friends, Peter, family, and yourself. As you do this, you will notice a large imbalance. Start to shift the hours of your day. Balance is what we are striving for.

"I also invite you to examine your thoughts. I see too much time consumed with getting the job done and not enough time recognizing the work that you have accomplished and reveling in the life you have. Does that make sense?"

"Totally."

"And finally, you will marry Peter. You just have to give him enough time to ask you!"

Diane laughs. I send her off, hoping she'll take my advice. I can see she'll be a lot happier if she does.

Forty minutes later, I am in a red two-door sporty thing, a rental car with 12 miles on the odometer and a CD player in the dash, speeding uptown to pick up David. I am euphoric.

"Cute car!" David exclaims as he walks out of our apartment building and heads over to give me a kiss.

"So cute, right? How was your day?"

David's a makeup artist. Call me a geek, but I think there's something really funny about the fact that he spends his days talking about colors people can use to highlight their best attributes, whereas I talk about the colors they carry around with them all the time. (And let me tell you, they're not always the most flattering. Do you know how hard it is to tell a football-loving salesman from Georgia that his aura is pink?) After trading shop talk, we spend the rest of the car ride singing to a bootleg copy of Ashlee Simpson (I'm not about to be caught actually buying that CD in the store) and preparing emotionally to move from city mentality to the country mentality of Cutchogue, New York.

On this particular night, as we pull up to my dad's country club, I cannot help but feel like we are preparing to infiltrate a secret society whose headquarters happen to be on the eastern end of Long Island. My sister and her husband are in town, my grandmother is visiting from Florida, and my father is eager to show us all off at his club.

Compared with most clubs, the North Fork Country Club is fairly modest. No valet, but they do adhere to a dress code. Not jacket and tie, but to the members of the NFCC, collarless shirts and denim are an *outrage*.

David and I sit in the parking lot, and I give him a little pep talk. (Actually, the talk is more for me.) Once we set foot in the club, we won't be able to move two inches without someone from my past greeting us. Family friends, neighbors—everybody and anybody is usually there, sniffing for new gossip. As we stare at the front door, I start to feel great pride that I am about to go in there with my head held high as an openly gay professional psychic with my Jewish boyfriend.

We walk through the front door, and there's an eerie silence, more like a church than a restaurant. We head straight for the bar to meet our host. Behold, my father, in all of his glory. In any crush of people, he is always easy to find. He stands next to my grandmother and aunt, wearing yellow pants and a blaringly loud plaid shirt. I meet his eyes and grin—I can't help but adore him. When I was a child, his choice of attire used to send me diving for antidepressants, yet as an adult, I can tell that his way of dressing really suits him.

I am also keenly aware that I myself am wearing a bright pink shirt.

My parents have been divorced for over 15 years, yet I still feel a brief bubble of pain that my mother is not with us. I leave David with my family and quickly place our drink order—two sour apple martinis. Once our drinks are placed safely in front of me, I breathe and start to feel a little more relaxed; I am fairly certain I don't know anyone in the room. For a moment, I stare at my lime green cocktail. For someone who doesn't want to stick out in this crowd, perhaps I should have selected another beverage. You know, something the good old boys would drink, like scotch or beer or—

"There is our movie star!"

Before I can take even one sip of my drink, a family friend is speeding toward me—an older, well-dressed woman with her husband in tow.

"How is the clairvoyant? I saw you on television—you were wonderful!"

"Thank you."

"Why weren't you able to tell me that this last year was going to be horrendous?"

I laugh nervously.

"Do you ever see anything bad?"

"Sometimes I do."

"Well, I don't want to know anything! Unless you can give me the lottery numbers!" She laughs hysterically at her own joke.

"Did you know she was going to say that?" her husband chimes in.

"Hi, Mr. Tate," I say politely.

Mr. and Mrs. Tate lived on the block where I grew up. Nice couple, friendly family. They haven't a clue about what I really do for a living. To them, I am like the Amazing Kreskin. Able to guess how much change is in your pocket, pull your name out of thin air, or correctly choose the card you are thinking of. As we stand around exchanging pleasantries, I try to divert the conversation from my work to their grandchildren. This only works for a minute—soon we are back to my mysterious job.

"So, what kind of things do you tell people?" Mrs. Tate asks. She is genuinely interested. "And how long are you on that psychic line during the day?"

I graciously try to mask my mortification. I do not work for a psychic hotline. (Okay, admittedly, I did it as a teenager, but that was a long time ago. We'll get to that later.)

"Mrs. Tate, I am more like a counselor. I see and talk to people about their problems. Then I make predictions on the outcome of certain situations in their lives."

"Well, I think it's great, just great!"

I smile and nod my head, and when they don't get the hint, I make a quick move with my body that forces them out of the way without them realizing I'd done it. I try not to use my 6'6" height too often—just in emergencies like this one. With a quick wave, I'm gone.

It's not that I dislike Mr. and Mrs. Tate. The fact is, it's fairly common that people don't understand what I do. Even I have a hard time explaining that I am not your ordinary psychic. I can talk to the dead, but I prefer not to. My goal is to help you understand why you are on this planet. Are you joyous? Are your needs being fulfilled? Are you embracing the simple things? Sure, predicting the outcome of loves and careers can be exciting, but my true goal is to make sure you are living your best possible life.

It's always a challenge for me to explain to the Mrs. Tates of the world exactly what it is I actually do and how on earth I got there. It's actually kind of a funny story, if you have a minute.

Chapter Two

MINI-MERLIN

As a kid, soccer was the bane of my existence. Garden City, Long Island, where I grew up, is a sports-crazed suburb. From a very early age, my friends would move every season from soccer in the spring to Little League in the summer, then football in the fall and ice hockey in the winter. I, on the other hand, did not have one athletic bone in my body. I was not interested in playing or even attending any of these games, but my mother forced me to choose at least one sport to participate in. I found that soccer left room for daydreaming, and there were a couple of positions that required little physical activity.

I used to stand my ground during the endless games and observe the dozen other boys on my team. We all wore black cleats with knee-high socks pulled over our shin guards. Our golden shirts shined in the warm spring sun, and the playing fields were perfectly green and manicured. The other boys took their positions seriously, standing in the fighter's stance with their feet shoulder-width apart. All I ever cared about was that if we won, we got ice cream.

This is Garden City to me: endless athletic events, cheering parents, mothers wearing pressed khaki pants and sensible short-sleeved tops. Parking lots full of Jeep Grand Cherokees, the hot new yuppie car. A safe, secure suburban life.

Don't get me wrong—it's a beautiful town. Towering oak trees line the streets. Manicured lawns, stately homes, accented shutters—many would call it picture-perfect. But that's just the problem. Most people in Garden City live in a certain kind of home, have a certain kind of job, and want to lead a certain kind of life. Everyone is relatively the same and strives to fit in. If you don't fit the mold, it can be a lonely place to grow up.

My dad had done what many people raised in Garden City do: leave for the first time to go away to school, decide they can't live without home, and return to marry, raise a family, and lead a comfortable, predictable life in their hometown. When you grow up in Garden City, you either love it or hate it—and the ones who hate it can't wait to get out and never look back. I was destined to be in the second group. From the very start, I just did not fit in.

From the outside, we were just another typical upper-middle-class family in a four-bedroom house, a mom who stayed home with my older sister, Tarrin, and me, and a station wagon in the driveway. Both my parents were the kind of adults everyone called by their first names. Ours was the cool house, the one where all the neighborhood kids liked to hang out. Every home on my street was pristine and tastefully decorated, except for ours. Our parents would nail 60 hats from the 1920s to a wall just because they thought it was fun. The Fraser family idea of recreation was to rearrange the furniture. My dad would swap out the living room furniture with the den and vice versa whenever he got bored. There was a whole different, loose vibe to our house.

We had a small, fenced-in backyard. The fence was just tall enough to keep our dogs from jumping out, but just low enough to comply with the strict Garden City zoning laws. God forbid anyone had a fence taller than 4 feet; that would be tacky. My father, in a trademark Bob Vila attempt, had laid his own redbrick patio in our yard. You had to love the man for his effort, but the finished product was far from smooth. While the patios at my friends' homes had been professionally laid out so that each brick was perfectly aligned side by side, our patio resembled the outfall of an earthquake. Nonetheless, our yard got the most use.

We were the only family on the block who ate dinner outside, but my dad was adamant about dining alfresco in the summertime. One night as the four of us ate and caught up on our days, we were greeted by a few raindrops from the sky.

"Dougall, it's raining, honey," my mother said to my dad. "Maybe we should move inside."

"It's a sun shower—I wouldn't worry about it," my dad responded.

Moments later, the rain really picked up. We all began to giggle as the water plopped into our glasses and bounced off our glass tabletop. My dad ran into the house and reappeared seconds later, carrying four umbrellas. He handed one to each of us, then sat in his seat, opened his umbrella, and continued to eat. We all shared a giggle and happily continued eating our soggy dinner.

ON THE OUTSIDE, IT LOOKED LIKE FUN. Free and easy, lots of laughs and good times. My mother was so open to everything in life. I think a large part of why I'm psychic is due to her and the way she nurtured me. She is the most liberal, accepting woman in the world. (If I were a matchmaker, I could not have thought of a less perfect match than my parents; perhaps that's why they are no longer together. My father is a Republican—excuse me while I hide my head in shame. I love you, Dad, but c'mon!)

My mother was a breath of fresh air in our little town. She neglected to wear shoes on special occasions. She used words like *shmatte* (Yiddish for "housedress"), though we were Christian. Dinner was always spicy. Any and all prejudice got stamped out of us early. She wouldn't stand for any racist or sexist comments. My mother was the only woman on the block who would round the corner sneaking a cigarette in her car and blasting old-school Madonna with the windows rolled down. No AC for this woman—she was having a "moment." When she pulled up in our driveway, she would make the car dance for me by stomping on the brake repeatedly in time to the rhythm. Part of me was consumed with embarrassment, but secretly I was devoted to her.

And she kept the house full of cheer—the common thread of the Fraser home was laughter. She was warm and loving and accepting . . . sometimes a little too accepting. I had a teenage babysitter named Tom, and the first time he did something inappropriate, I went running to my mom. "Tom did weird things last night," I told her. "He showed me magazines with naked ladies, and I didn't like it."

My mom told me, "It's normal for young men to look at magazines like that." So I went off to bed that night thinking that what Tom had done was a normal, correct way to behave. My mom had said so, right? It happened again, I spoke to my mom again, and once more I was told that Tom was behaving normally. As a 7-year-old, I didn't have the vocabulary to say, "I'm being touched inappropriately." The right words just weren't there. I was a kid who was aware enough to know that something was not right and aware enough to go to my parents and say, "I don't like this." But Mom didn't seem overly concerned, so the next time it happened, I kicked Tom in the face. Hard. He never touched me again. My parents were great fun, and I certainly always knew I was loved and cared for, but I had an early sense that I was going to have to take care of myself.

From the start, I was a troubled, chubby, angry little boy. I used to tear my hair out, throw things at my mother, write in my little diary about how I wanted to die. Can you say "drama"? Certainly I was insecure. Who wasn't? And yes, I had some anger issues—lots of kids did. But many of my antics were purely for attention. If I had really wanted to kill myself, I probably would have. I just wanted the focus to be all me, all the time. The slightest lack of focus on me personally would set me right off.

One night after dinner, my father informed me it was time for me to do the dishes.

> **I certainly always knew I was loved and cared for, but I had an early sense that I was going to have to take care of myself.**

"Dougall, it's your turn."

"Yes, I know it's my turn, but can't the maid do them tomorrow?"

"'Maid'?" This was just the kind of thing that made my mother mad. "She is the *domestic engineer*."

"The domestic what?"

"You will refer to her by her first name or as the domestic engineer."

I stared down at our tablecloth—which resembled something Mrs. Roper would wear—and realized I was losing this battle. Grumpily I took the dirty dishes into the kitchen. Vigorously sulking, I placed the dishes in the dishwasher and listened to the laughter from the dining room. My sister, Tarrin, and a couple of her friends who were always at our house were joking and laughing with my parents, not missing me at all. This infuriated me. I stared down at the utensils and picked up a knife. I grabbed the handle of the blade, pointed it toward my stomach, and waited. Checking my reflection in the window, I satisfied myself that I looked appropriately determined. I adjusted my stance ever so slightly so that when someone entered the room, they would immediately be faced with my death tableau, in either the reflection or, better yet, the flesh. This would show them. No dishes for me!

A couple of minutes passed. The hilarity in the dining room continued. After about 10 minutes of waiting for someone to come along and witness my horrid threat of suicide, I decided that finishing the dishes was a faster way to get back to the fun already in progress in the other room.

❧ YOU MIGHT SAY I WAS A PROFOUNDLY SENSITIVE CHILD. When I was happy, I was ecstatic. I took pleasure in the smaller things in life. Superheroes were my best friends. My particular favorite was Wonder Woman. Man or woman, straight or gay, Wonder Woman was just cool. I was lucky to have a mother who wanted her children to express themselves fully. As a boy, I was allowed to watch and worship the bathing suit–clad superheroine. I kid you not, I practically burned a hole in our carpet, spinning around just waiting for my own radical change. The living room became a blur as I prayed that in a flash I would be transformed.

Superheroes in general were very interesting to me. Wonder Woman had amazing strength and kick-ass boots. The Bionic Man was hired by the government to solve crimes. Caine from *Kung Fu* was not exactly a superhero, but he adhered to a strict regimen of spirituality and martial arts. And then there was Aquaman, who had special skills and could live on either land or water. My overriding memory of him? He always wore a tight orange shirt that caressed every muscle of his manly chest. With his wavy blond hair, he was a god to me. I was a bit perplexed by my instinctive attraction to Aquaman. I knew I didn't want to be him—I just wanted to be *close* to him.

My little soul was confused, so I immersed myself in cartoons and other worlds for direction. I was also a dirty little kid; I refused to bathe on any regular schedule, and my teachers often resorted to calling our house, telling my mother, "Your child is grimy." They were right. My hair was dirty and never combed. There was always dirt under my fingernails, and my clothes were grungy. Wonder Woman wouldn't be caught dead swinging the lasso of truth without every hair in place; yet here I was, showering maybe biweekly at best. My parents took it in stride. They even teased me about it, which only made me angrier.

And anger was my real problem. My temper was no joke—it was fierce and sudden. I was that kid you see screaming in a mall and you think to yourself, *His parents must be torturing him.* No, I'm afraid I was torturing them. It was awful. I broke things—there were quite a few replacement windows in our house. I hurled stuff to express my rage. The smallest thing could set me off. Basically, I was Damien.

Seeing that Wonder Woman and Aquaman were busy fighting crime, I took solace in my imaginary friend. "Imaginary" was the label given Doshun by my parents. But to me he was quite real. Doshun was my proof, and continues to sustain my belief, that all kids see and sense things beyond the physical realm, but this ability slowly diminishes as they grow up. Doshun, a big pink ball of light, was my constant companion. He was a well-established part of all our lives; we set a place for him at the table and everything. Nearly every kid goes through the stage of having an imaginary friend, but I took it further than most. Doshun came with me wherever I went; he comforted me when my parents argued or my sister was too busy for me. He was the

> My imaginary
> friend was my proof,
> and continues to
> sustain my belief,
> that all kids see
> and sense things
> beyond the
> physical realm.

perfect companion. He always agreed with me, he didn't roughhouse and make messes in the house, and he eventually wormed his way into my family's affections. Neighborhood kids had the audacity to question his existence. Peons.

"Can Dougall come out and play, Mrs. Fraser?"

"Do! James is here and he wants to play."

Now, James was fun and all, and sure, he was a real, flesh-and-blood kid clearly visible to everyone, but he had so many opinions.

"I think I'll just stay home and play with Doshun, Mom."

"Do, now, you know I love Dosh, but don't you think it would be more fun to go outside for a bit and play with . . . um . . . *real* kids?"

"M-o-m-m-m! Dosh *is* real!"

What did she know? All the other kids' imaginary friends had gradually died off, but I was eager to hold on to mine for a little bit longer. This soon became another ongoing battle. Mom said I needed to play with real people, though I was perfectly content. But alas, I would succumb to society's outright prejudice toward unseen friends.

"Fine, I'll play with James." Big sigh. How pedestrian. But at least James always wanted to play GI Joe.

Under pressure, I finally let Doshun die and did my best to make friends with the other living children in the area. I was actually doing a fairly good job until the summer after first grade. In Garden City, you were either doing well or flat-out rich. Most of my friends headed off with their families to the Hamptons every summer. My family did not have a vacation house at the beach. So for one last summer, I decided that Doshun would reincarnate.

It was a hot August day, and I was bored out of my mind. The street was desolate. I needed a friend, and I swear I remember looking down the street and seeing that familiar pink light hovering nearby, begging to approach me.

"*Doshun!*" I screamed. "Mom, look—it's Doshun!"

"I thought Dosh died?" my mom asked.

"He did, but he's back," I said with some exasperation. "People do come back, you know!"

Was it possible that I had been singled out as a child to have a remarkable connection to greater knowledge and all things spiritual and divine? Unlikely. Did my mother listen to me and go along with me and nurture my imagination? Absolutely. Whether I was bringing my so-called imaginary pink light back to life or immersing myself in cartoons and marveling at the accomplishments of superheroes, my imagination and creativity were given free rein. I was supported and loved.

As much as I adored my pink ball of light, he was kind of a submissive friend—he'd never challenge me on anything! By the time I was in second grade, Doshun went the way of the cast-aside former best pal.

One night my mom started telling me about the fun she'd had with her college roommates, contacting ghosts and "the other side." I was fascinated by these stories and begged for more. She pulled out a brand-new Ouija board, and, giggling, we unwrapped the box and read from the almighty scripture of Mattel. Setting the board up in between us, we followed the directions religiously. I closed my eyes and sat patiently, awaiting a message from the spirit world. My mother's silver bracelets jingled distractingly in the background as I tried to concentrate. My chubby fingers trembled on the pointer—I was sure we'd soon be speaking to the other side.

"Will it rain tomorrow?" Mom asked loudly. Nothing happened.

"It's not working!" I screamed.

"It's just a toy, Do."

But to me it was much more than a toy. I fully believed it was possible that a game manufacturer came up with this brilliant tool to contact the spirit world. Despite the lack of results from the Ouija board, I decided that I would explore this whole idea of contacting the other side much further. But it needed to be done right.

The next afternoon, I concocted my own plan and gathered the proper tools. James had come over again, and I informed him that we would not be playing GI Joe or Cops and Robbers today. This afternoon we would be expanding our minds. We were going to hold a séance.

The first order of business was protection. Now, what would protect us from evil spirits? Holy water? Where on earth would I get holy water? I grabbed a spray bottle from the guest bathroom and prayed over it, mumbling nonsense words that I thought sounded spiritual and powerful. After dousing the room in my makeshift holy water, I moved to my next step: mood lighting. I inverted the blinds to create a dim, spooky atmosphere that would be inviting to the spirit world. James, of course, was no help. He just sat on my carpet with a confused look on his face as I raced around in a fever of activity.

"Who should we contact?" I asked him excitedly.

"Why are we doing this?"

"Because."

"Because why?"

Aghast at his lack of interest, I blurted out, "Just do it, James!"

This was serious business! I had a flash of inspiration. "I know. We'll contact Abe Lincoln!" He was the most famous dead person I could imagine with an instantly recognizable face; it just seemed an appropriate choice. I grabbed a penny—Abe's calling card, so to speak.

I was after far more proof than a plastic piece on a game board answering my yes-or-no questions. I wanted nothing less than for Abe to call me on the phone. As James and I sat in the dark with a candle lit and my portable phone inverted so its green light would shine on the penny, I felt like a genius.

"*I call upon the presence of Abe Lincoln!* Abe, please make your presence known! Make the phone ring, and speak to me!"

Seconds passed. Silence. Abe was apparently not taking calls.

James was bored. We soon gave up and ran outside to play GI Joe. But I was hooked. I spent many hours alone in my room in the glow of the portable phone, trying to summon Abe Lincoln. I knew there was something on the other side—I just had to reach it.

꧁ **MY AUNT GAIL WAS OUR FAMILY HIPPIE,** given to wearing ponchos and fingerless gloves in any weather. As a kid, I thought she was the coolest person in the world. She said "Shit!" and "Fuck!" all the time, right in front of me. She was a big talker with a great sense of humor, and she was very independent. She'd been married and divorced twice, or was it three times? When she entered a room, people were instantly captivated or offended by her strong views, which she was not shy about expressing. Like my mother, she had a strong sense of social justice and was a committed liberal.

She lived in a great old house with hundreds of antique books and huge, dramatic paintings on the walls. One piece that particularly in-

I knew there was something on the other side—I just had to reach it.

trigued me as a child was a paint tin, with the brush stuck randomly in the dried paint, hung up on her wall as a "piece." This was just the kind of thing she was into. You were not to laugh at it because it was Art, and Art was very important. Aunt Gail was always racing off to see foreign films and art shows. I was 6 or 7 years old, sitting next to her watching an Italian movie with subtitles, which wasn't exactly fun at the time, but her intentions were good. She wanted to open my eyes to the important things in life: culture and beauty and art. I worshipped her.

It was Aunt Gail's idea to take my mother and me on a day trip to Lily Dale, which was virtually in her backyard. Lily Dale is a small community in southwest New York, about an hour away from Buffalo. Its residents have been dedicated to spiritualism for 125 years. Open to the public only in the summer, it's a charming little 19th-century psychic village, where residents have to audition to be allowed to live there. Community standards are high—if a resident receives too many complaints, they are asked to leave.

All I knew was that my mom and aunt were going to a special place to get psychic readings. I was totally excited about our excursion. The town itself was lovely, with old-fashioned two-story homes with screened-in porches. We wandered around the storybook village and rested in the park. The only things that tipped visitors to the fact that this wasn't just another sleepy little village were the signs in every window advertising each owner's specialty.

My aunt liked one particular psychic, whom she had visited several times and wanted to see again. My mom told me to pick whichever house I wanted, and we'd both get a reading. I chose a yellow house, and Mom and I walked up and rang the doorbell. An older woman came to the door with her hair tied severely back in a bun. She wasn't conventionally pretty, but there was something striking about her. She was very soft-spoken and wore exactly what I imagined a psychic should wear—a long, flowing gypsy skirt and big earrings. She was everything a kid would want a psychic to be.

"We'd like to get two readings," my mom told her.

The psychic turned her huge eyes on me and looked me up and down. I was a chubby, grubby kid wearing Hawaiian board shorts and a T-shirt printed with the words "Hang Loose." My T-shirt was tight, meant for a kid who surfed all day, not for a kid who ate Cheetos all day. She shook her head. "I'm sorry. I can't read for him. I don't read for children."

"All right," Mom replied. She understood; she was fine with it. She was going to get her reading—what did she care? I crumpled with disappointment. But then the woman looked at me again and cocked her head to the side.

"No, I will read for him, but I'll only do it for half price."

"Half price" didn't sound good to my 8-year-old ears. Did that mean she wasn't going to tell me everything she saw? The whole idea threw me off a little—I didn't expect a visionary to be bargaining.

"No, I want the whole thing, the real deal!" I said. (Now I understand the psychic's hesitation. In real life, when you read for a younger kid, once you've established that Jimmy in your math club likes you, there's only so much further you can take it. I was, after all, only 8.)

Mom and I waited on the porch while she finished up with another client. It was a beautiful summer day, hot and sunny. The chimes on the front porch tinkled in the breeze. I was consumed with excitement. Once we entered, my first thought was that the old yellow house smelled like a garage sale. Dusty, basement-y . . . not bad, exactly, but there was certainly a musty odor to the room. Finally we walked into a very small room with wood paneling where the psychic was sitting on a small love seat. Leaving my mom in the next room, I sat down in a chair facing the psychic. It was very dark in the room, and she cranked up a big, old-fashioned timer and set it at 20 minutes. She put the timer down, and it started clicking away as she closed her eyes and lowered her head almost to her chest. Two minutes later, very dramatically and suddenly, her head popped back up. I was on the edge of my seat, mesmerized. Clearly, the spirits had arrived.

She looked to her left, then back at me. "Your grandparents are on a trip."

"No they're not!" I contradicted, very bratty.

She looked to her left again and nodded to herself. "Yes they are. Your grandparents are on a trip, and they will bring something back for you. It will mean a great deal to them, but it won't make any sense to you."

How disappointing. This was my psychic reading?

She looked to her left again. "You have quite a temper. You are surrounded by a red wall of anger."

I stopped fidgeting and grew very still. That got my attention.

"There are spirits trying to contact you. If you can work on your anger and control your temper, you can help a lot of people." She looked to the left again, then back at me. "You're going to be a phil-anthropist." Then, ding, the bell went off and our reading was over. "Our time is up."

"Why do you look to the left?" I was dying to know.

"Because I'm looking into the spirit world."

Wow. We got up, and then it was my mother's turn for a reading. I pulled on her arm as she was walking toward the reading room. "Don't tell her anything, Mom! Don't tell her you're my mom!" Trying to fool the psychic, as if she couldn't figure that one out on her own.

When my mom came out of her reading, I dragged her off to the gift store so I could buy a crystal. I was full of energy, bouncing all over the place. We rejoined my aunt and started driving home. "What's a philanthropist, what's a philanthropist?" I kept asking.

"We'll look it up in the dictionary when we get home, Dougall, but a philanthropist is a person who is very wealthy and does good things with their money."

I was thrilled. Forget doing good things; all I heard was lots of money. I sat back the rest of the ride and thought about the psychic telling me that the spirits were trying to contact me. I immediately envisioned a Native American spirit guide. I could see the feather; I could hear the flute music. Don't ask me where this vision came from; it just popped into my head out of nowhere. My mom and aunt would go see a psychic, sure, but they weren't that into all things New Age. But I liked the vision, and I was positive a Native American spirit guide would soon be contacting me.

I called my dad the minute we got back to my aunt's house. "I went to the psychic today, and the psychic said that Gamma and Poppy were on a trip."

"They are on a trip, to Scotland," Dad told me.

"She said they got me a gift I wasn't going to understand."

"They did get you a gift," Dad said, "but you'll have to wait and see what it is."

I didn't actually receive the gift until a couple of months later. When my grandparents returned from their extended trip and came to visit our family, they presented me with a tie made of the Fraser tartan, the Scottish plaid.

The psychic had predicted correctly. I couldn't have cared less about the tie. I was too young to understand the great pride my father's family took in their Scottish heritage. What struck me was that the psychic had been right. She knew.

I remembered what she had said about the wall of anger surrounding me. That night as I lay in bed, I pictured myself surrounded

The psychic had predicted correctly. I was too young to understand, but what struck me was that the psychic had been right. She knew.

by a tall brick wall. The bricks were red and transparent, and I imagined my small self huddled inside four walls that went over my head. I envisioned myself reaching up high, taking one of the bricks off the top row, and throwing it off the wall as far as I could. I went around in a circle, brick by brick by brick, until all of them were gone. When all the bricks had been tossed and the wall was gone, I pictured friendly Native American spirits coming to sit around me and talk with me.

I started putting myself to sleep this way every night. It was my first use of creative visualization and working with energy in my head. No one told me to picture each red brick of anger coming down. I just did it. But that is how energy works—and I instinctively knew it. The redbrick wall of anger was a very apt image—because that wall was keeping people from me.

Chapter Three

THE LIGHT AT THE END
OF THE TUNNEL

AN ALL-TOO TYPICAL SCENE FROM MY CHILDHOOD: My sister and her friends are practicing for cheerleading auditions in our foyer. I sit on our staircase, watching them throw their arms and tighten their stance in an ecstasy of school spirit. Huddled on our pea green carpeted stairs, I am positive I can hit the marks with more pizzazz than Tarrin.

"Dougall, go outside and play!" Tarrin shouts.

"I wanna watch!"

"Tarrin! Let your brother watch!" my mom screams. My parents are arguing in the kitchen. My mother is always trying to force Tarrin and me to spend more time together. Looking back, I have to wonder if she was projecting her lack of quality time with my dad on the two of us.

I was born 8 years after my sister, Tarrin, and because of the large gap in our ages, we weren't particularly close growing up. I adored her from afar as a child. She was a teenager; she was cool. Naturally she couldn't have cared less about me. When I was 8 and Tarrin 16, she suddenly started bruising very easily. Overnight, her body became covered with horrible purple bruises. A rush

> My sister, in her own way, was very spiritual; she believed that she had created the cancer in her own body.

visit to the doctor and several days of testing brought stunning news: Tarrin had cancer.

The leukemia was caught very early, and she was given an excellent prognosis. Tarrin, in her own way, was very spiritual; she believed that she had created the cancer in her own body. My parents' marriage was rocky; my mom had started to drop hints about leaving. When Tarrin was diagnosed with leukemia, it put a quick stop to any talk of separation. How could you even think about such a thing when your daughter had cancer?

It was while Tarrin was battling leukemia that we grew really close for the first time. Nothing like a death threat to make you appreciate your big sister. But I was still an angry little brat not above using my sister's illness to get what I wanted. Which was to stay out of school. Her cancer was pretty handy sometimes. I'd wake up and say to my mother with big doe eyes, "I want to know what's happening to Tarrin at the hospital," just so I didn't have to go to school. Of course, I would always be allowed to go with my parents to see her.

We handled the crisis in our usual family way—we pulled together and joked around a lot. The whole time Tarrin was sick, the three of us called her "Luke" (short for leukemia). We took turns trying on her wig—I think it looked best on my dad. We'd be sitting in a room full of bald kids and their parents, and we'd be the only group that was laughing. Hysterically. For a short while, I was assigned a therapist who worked with the siblings of cancer patients. She pulled out her little puppets, and I was supposed to tell Cancer Cat puppet how Tarrin's illness made me feel. All I could think of when I heard her voice was the Peanuts cartoons in which all the adults sound like "Mwah, mwah, mwah." She made no sense to me; I couldn't believe this helped any kids.

School was always a problem zone for me. I spent a lot of time in the principal's office for "disorderly conduct," which included such offenses as calling teachers by their first names and "acting out" in fits of temper. No "Mrs. Smith" for me—I preferred "Susie." I went to a lot of trouble to find out my teachers' first names.

My antics in the classroom were well-received by my peers. It became my private crusade to make the entire room laugh whenever possible. On one particular day in fifth grade, we were lining up outside our room for lunch.

"Class, I want you all to line up single file! And no talking!" Mrs. Smith announced.

I took my favorite place, last. Chatting away to Jen in front of me. Jen was a goody two-shoes, so she remained silent.

"Hands down and mouths closed! That means you, Dougall!"

Mrs. Smith slowly began to walk in my direction.

"I said, '*Hands down and mouths closed*'!!!"

As she approached me, the entire class turned around to look in my direction. I couldn't let her win, so I slowly opened my mouth and raised my right hand high in the air.

Mrs. Smith angrily grabbed my arm. "Dougall, listen to me! Why don't you listen to me?"

"Susie, what's your problem?"

I was quickly sent to the principal's office. Again.

Soon after that, my parents told me I was going to see a special doctor every week for some real therapy. My anger was still quite a problem; the stress of Tarrin's illness on all of us exacerbated my already terrible temper. I was happy to go because whatever they were calling "therapy" would get me out of school early.

I started seeing my therapist once a week. He quickly grew to know all the Frasers quite well. My mother had been his first client, literally coming in for her first session the very day he opened his practice. My father joined her for couples counseling a few times, and Tarrin saw him intermittently for issues relating to her illness, but my mother and I became his long-term regular patients.

I thought the doctor was a bit of a nut job himself. He always had coffee breath and would munch pastries during our session, and the crumbs would lodge in his mustache. Even though I was just a child, I felt it was inappropriate that he was eating during my time.

I liked leaving school early every Thursday. I felt "special." In fact, therapy seemed like more fun than most of the things adults made me do until the day I bumped into Amy, a classmate, in the waiting room. The look of pure panic on both mothers' faces when Amy and I saw each other was hysterical. In the car on the way home, my mother admonished me in her sternest tone "not to tell anyone" that I'd seen Amy or that either one of us was a patient of that particular doctor.

Telling me "don't" was the best way to make sure I did something. If my mother had ignored the meeting, I wouldn't have said a word. But she was so adamant when she said, "Do not tell anyone about this!" that I couldn't wait to tell everyone at school the next day.

I quickly discovered that Amy and I weren't the only two kids from our school seeing a shrink. In fact, there were quite a few of us who'd been told not to discuss our weekly sessions. Both my mother and

Amy's mother were very nervous that their child's after-school activity would be revealed. I can't blame them for wanting to protect us; it was a slightly shameful secret to parents who came from the piano-lessons-after-school generation. But I grew up in the my-kid's-in-therapy-or-on-Ritalin generation and had no compunction about spreading the story all over school. I thought the whole thing was funny.

It wasn't quite so funny when it eventually dawned on me that I wasn't going to "therapy" so I could play games with a nice, well-meaning man. Yes, it meant I was special, but not in a good way. I was there because something was seriously wrong with me. I knew that already! I was chubby, I was angry, I didn't bathe, my parents were unhappily married, my grades were miserable, and my sister had cancer. She might even die. Yes, I had quite a few problems. I knew none of the adults in my life could help me, either. My mother in particular was going through her own crisis.

My mom had always been a large woman, in an attractive, Star Jones kind of way. My dad was the hearty, successful real estate agent who looked fine, even distinguished, with a few extra pounds. I used to watch my mom getting ready to go to parties. First she'd try a hairstyle I called "the Governor's Wife," pulling it all back with a headband. Then she'd make a sound of disgust and arrange her hair into an elaborate bun, with the same result. It would go back and forth for

> **I was chubby, I was angry, I didn't bathe, my parents were unhappily married, my grades were miserable, and my sister had cancer. Yes, I had quite a few problems.**

a while—bun, headband, bun, headband.... Then she'd start crying.

Same thing with her outfit. Whenever she went out, she'd try on every possible combination in her closet before settling on the same brown dress again. I used to wonder, *Why not just put on the brown dress and save half an hour?* She always told me that I was beautiful and special, but the way she looked at herself resonated with me in a way that her loving words did not.

> **My mom always told me that I was beautiful and special, but the way she looked at herself resonated with me in a way that her loving words did not.**

When Tarrin's health crisis was over—once my sister had gone into remission and life could pretty much return to normal—Mom went on strike. "I'm over it.... I don't want to make lunches anymore. You all expect me to do all the cooking and cleaning and laundering. I have other things to do with my life. I am officially finished with all that."

Once she'd emancipated herself, she threw herself into volunteer work and immediately made an impact on a group of people whose lives were on the edge. "Accepting" does not begin to cover her unconditionally loving attitude. At the soup kitchen in the next town over, she easily befriended crack whore trannies, who soon felt quite comfortable calling our house. I grew accustomed to getting collect calls for my mom. She became quite well-known as the Long Island housewife who waded right into homeless shelters and dropped her Fendi bag into the pile with everyone else's paper shopping bag. And all the people in the soup kitchens and shelters liked her and trusted her and never once stole from her bag. She particularly bonded with a group of eight homeless men from El Salvador. Tarrin, Dad, and I called them "the Guys."

I used to come home from school and open the kitchen door, only to be greeted by El Salvadoran music blaring from the kitchen stereo. The stench of dirt and sweat would make my stomach heave. But my mother would be sitting right there, glaring at me with a look that said, "Don't you dare make these people feel uncomfortable." So I would sit at the table next to Miguel and pretend it was totally normal to share my Capri Sun with a 40-year-old homeless man.

She used to let the Guys come to our home and take showers every few months or so, which was really scary to me. My mom brushed aside any reservations by accusing the rest of us of being judgmental. "These are normal human beings, and you are going to accept them." I certainly learned a lesson about acceptance and giving, but I had to wonder if this was appropriate behavior on her part. Dad wasn't sure either. When we held family meetings, he would lay down the law: He was supportive of her soup kitchen work, but this was over the line. "No more homeless people in the house." That rule never stuck.

Family meetings always started because there were cups and glasses all over the house. It was my mom's biggest complaint. Then talk usually turned to a discussion of my horrible temper, but now we had bigger concerns. My mom was missing family dinners because Jambo had the flu. The phone was constantly ringing with collect calls from prison. It was all just bizarre, but my dad had been chastened by my mom's refusals to cooperate, and by this time my sister and I had been vigorously conditioned to be tolerant, kind people. So we just pretended it was normal to have a guy who was out of prison for the day at our dinner table.

Things were certainly changing. My mother was on her own new quest—she was certainly seeking to walk a new path. None of us liked it, but we all ignored it. My sister and I never talked about how weird Mom was being, just acted as if everything was all right.

Tarrin had her own concerns; she had missed a great deal of school the year she had leukemia and wanted only to graduate and put high school behind her. She took off as soon as she could for college in Boston. I was now alone in the house with my unhappy parents and, along with all my other problems, had to suffer through the pains of adolescence. And there were many.

IN JUNIOR HIGH, I WAS ACTUALLY FAIRLY POPULAR. Garden City students enter junior high in the sixth grade. It was the first year we received letter grades. Ms. Olsen was my sixth-grade teacher and the only teacher, to this day, whom I did not call by her first name. Let's just say she let me do a report on ESP and I loved her. I got an A in her class, and I'm pretty sure it was the last A I ever got. With each successive school year, my popularity slowly diminished. My male friends had the audacity to start dating. Can you believe it? We had been having so much fun on our own.

Suddenly everyone had a girlfriend. In junior high the term "girlfriend" was used quite loosely. When a pack of boys and girls went to the mall together, that was pretty much considered a "date" with your "girlfriend." But the closer we got to eighth grade, our final year of junior high, the more our bodies matured, and I had to face the fact that I was very different.

The summer after eighth grade, some friends had a big graduation party. The Kents lived on Snob Hill in what was by far the biggest house in Garden City. Huge and white, it was more like a country club than a private home. They had a wraparound porch, a large swimming pool, bedrooms out the yin yang; Susan Lucci was their neighbor. It was a very fancy, grown-up party. Well-dressed men walked around with champagne flutes filled with soda, but I had only one mission: a French kiss. It seemed everyone from the pack had started making out, and I was determined that I would not enter the ninth grade as the homo who had never kissed.

Under serious pressure, I sought out Cindy. It was the night before I left for camp, so I needed to move fast. With my voice cracking just the slightest bit, I asked her to go sit in the gazebo with me. Before she could even sit down, in an effort to prove my masculinity, I wrapped my sweaty palms around her and began to kiss her. (It was really more like resuscitation.) Surely this would prove I was a *man*.

We stayed locked together for what felt like eternity. And after 15 seconds of a boy trying to be a man, I could not figure out what the big fuss was all about. When our lip lock broke, rather than the professed feeling of satisfaction, I couldn't help but notice the flavor of her saliva in my mouth. A teenage mix of orange soda and pretzels.

"Was that your first time?" she asked.

Was it the sweaty palms or the poking tongue jab that gave me away? It was my first time, but I was certainly not going to let her know that. I needed a story—fast. In junior high, you can't lie about another classmate—eighth graders have their fact checkers, and I would be found out in no time. I needed a good camp story.

"No way, I had a girlfriend at camp last year. We made out all the time."

I slowly began to withdraw, busying myself with studying books about energy and colors and creative visualization. Anything to take me away.

Ironically, I went to an all-boy summer camp, but she didn't need to know that. Whatever happened to the good old days, a time when all you had to do was give a girl your pin and Rock Hudson was a "straight" role model? Those days were gone; now it was coed parties and spin the bottle. It was a nightmare.

In my spare time, I started reading books on my own. My mother was a bit of a self-help junkie. I would sit cross-legged on the wooden floor of my parents' bedroom and scan through the list of titles on her shelf. *Fat Is a Way of Life, Daring Divorce, What Color Is Your Parachute, Codependent No More,* . . . hmmm, *Medicine Woman* by Lynne Andrews—now, that book looked appealing! I slowly began to withdraw, busying myself with studying books about energy and colors and creative visualization. Anything to take me away.

It was clear to me that the only place I had power within my peer group was Camp Dudley. The oldest boys' summer camp in the United States, Camp Dudley in upstate New York was for years a great refuge for me. Dudley did not push athletics particularly hard. They had programs in drama and art and music, and the accommodations were hardly roughing it. We had working fireplaces in our cabins, and the food was incredible. Though I told my parents year after year that I didn't want to go, I really did. At camp I was able to be whoever I wanted to be.

This particular year, I was a counselor in training. We were known as aides. Each of us was the gofer of a cabin, and it was our responsibility to make sure that our campers kept their areas clean. One of the perks was that we got one night off a week. That meant that after taps, we were allowed to roam the campus until midnight. I had a select group of friends that came back every year, and we would spend our nights off ordering pizza and ignoring our curfew.

One evening, I was sitting on the ground near Avery Boathouse with five other 14-year-old boys—boys who used words like "masturbation," not "meditation." Brian casually asked me about what religion I was. I was shocked; given the setting, he couldn't have asked me anything more bizarre.

Suddenly, a beam of light about the circumference of a grapefruit shot down from the sky and landed on the ground beside me. Startled, I looked around at everyone, expecting them to be as terrified and confused as I was. But they just kept looking at me, waiting for me to answer the question as if nothing had happened. And then I understood: Nothing had happened for them. They didn't see the beam of light shining down from the sky into the ground next to me. It was not visible to them at all.

I didn't know what to say. I felt like God's flashlight was trained on me in that moment. If I mentioned the light, they would think I was crazy. (Was I? A familiar question!) From a distance, I heard myself say that recently I had been studying psychic phenomena.

Another beam of light, purple this time, flew down from the sky and landed on the other side of me. I was now surrounded by about 10 different shades of white, purple, and blue streams of light. Certainly I'd never experienced anything like this before, but I was in awe, not afraid, of the streaming lights. Still, I was sitting on the ground by a boathouse in the Adirondacks with five guys. I had to say something. Clumsily, I struggled to describe my experience with

> A blue light came out of the sky, hit me in the forehead and the chest, and filled my entire body with warmth. I was in awe, not afraid, of the streaming lights.

meditation, something I'd newly discovered and had been secretly practicing at camp.

They looked at me like I was on crack. One or two seemed actually frightened by what I was saying. Kyle triumphantly snorted, "I don't believe that stuff."

Then—whack! A blue light came out of the sky, hit me in the forehead and the chest, and filled my entire body with warmth. The spot on my forehead buzzed a little bit. I could feel everything, from the top of my head to the tips of my toes, all at once. My temperature spiked. I had never felt so intensely alive.

"I see lights," I said. "Do you see them? I feel lights. They just hit me."

My heart was pounding, and I was very nervous about my friends' reactions to my confession, not the lights. What would these guys think of me? They were going to tell everyone at camp that I was a freak. I already felt like enough of a freak without beams of light bouncing from the sky—and here, in the one place where I had some stature. They were quiet and still, watching me warily. Lit by the warmth of the blue light inside me, I closed my eyes—and a woman's face was looking at me. Oh, great, now I was seeing a woman in my fantasies! I opened my eyes. I couldn't see her anymore. When I closed my eyes, she appeared again. Now I was scared.

"White" cannot even begin to explain the glow transfusing her skin. She looked like Japanamation. Wearing a blue scarf on her head, she tilted her chin down to the left as she gazed steadfastly into my eyes. A crown of stars hovered around her head. In my thoughts, I asked her who she was. She responded, "I'm Mary."

Go away, I thought. She vanished.

Terrified, I opened my eyes. That vision of Mary scared me so much that I told everyone in detail what I was seeing. Mary. The lights coming from the sky. I didn't care that I sounded like a freak because I didn't want to feel alone. I needed to feel connected to them.

"Can't you see it? It's here! It's right here!" I pointed to the spots on the ground where the light was landing. Nobody else saw anything. They stared at me in amazement. I told them what I'd learned about energy and color—that the energy language of the universe was color.

"If you want to intensify or balance certain types of energy within yourself, you focus your attention on the energy, and that energy's color," I said. I was babbling. Kyle's eyebrow went up. I felt his disbelief and knew he was going to be the first to ridicule me, but I continued. I had to tell them what was going on with me. No, I had to keep talking to prevent Mary from returning. And then, just like that, my mind was filled with information about the boys in the circle around me.

I turned to Jason. Jason was the kind of guy who would choose Birkenstocks over duck shoes.

"Your parents criticize you constantly, don't they?" I asked.

"Excuse me?" he said, clearly flustered.

"I can feel your father yelling at you. He wants you to become a pro golfer, not a musician. He bullies you." I could literally feel his father's rage inside my body. "Jason, you don't have to choose. The arts are your destiny." He began to cry. "Your parents are wrong for trying to prevent you from fulfilling your destiny." I had never met Jason's parents. Actually, none of us spoke much about our families back home.

The four boys were sitting, slack-jawed, staring at me. They were absolutely stunned. Then Jason opened up. "That's so strange that you say that. Before I came here for the summer, I was arguing with my parents. They were yelling at me for the way that I dress, and my father was angry that I wouldn't take golf lessons with him." He hung his head and couldn't look directly at us. His voice choked up with emotion.

"I just feel like my dad has no idea who I am." He told us about the pressure he got from his family to be a pro golfer—and live out his father's dream. We all listened quietly. As he spoke, he began to calm down. The energy in my mind moved from him to the next person, Matt. His aura was a dark, dark purple.

"You fear God," I said. Now Matt burst into tears.

And then, just like that, my mind was filled with information about the boys in the circle around me. I started giving the first psychic readings of my life.

"When I go to church, I feel like I don't belong there," he said.

I can't remember what I said to him. The words poured out of my mouth. I know they were soothing words and they seemed to help him. I wanted him to feel safe. And I continued moving through the circle, giving the first psychic readings of my life. I was able to see, perceive, and hear inside my head intimate details about each boy's life.

I didn't understand what happened to me that night. I still don't, but I knew it was divine. I saw things that I'd never seen before. Some people believed me, and some didn't. Opinions and expectations of me changed, in some ways dramatically. But I did not rise to my feet afterward and walk across the lake on the top of the water. I did just the opposite—I went back to my cabin with a sense of fear inside me. Fear that I had seen something truly magnificent, and fear that I could not stop imagining the feel of Kevin's lips pressed against mine.

Chapter Four

FAST TIMES AT GURU HIGH

THERE WAS NO GOING BACK TO THE SIMPLE LIFE OF WEIRD DOUGALL AFTER THE VISION AT CAMP DUDLEY. I was Really Weird (and Probably Gay!) Dougall now. The respite of summer vacation over, I faced my biggest fear: school.

Adults like to think that school is a safe place where, as equals, we youths bow our innocent heads over our books to learn together. That's a bunch of crap. For me, school was war. I was an undercover agent. Double-0 gypsy. Wearing a medicine bag filled with crystals, I tried to dodge senior gaydar every day. My only weapons against their cruel assaults were sarcasm and wit—not enough firepower. I needed a decoy. Any teacher would do.

In biology class, for example, I made fun of Ruth—pardon me, Ms. Jones—to deflect the attention from me. Having gained a 45-minute reprieve from receiving personal pain by inflicting it, I basked in the glow of class laughter. I was truly leading a double life with my peers, who saw me as alternately the funny one or the fag. My teachers, however, just saw me as "rude." Now, of course, I agree with them. Yes, I am ashamed of some of the things I did to survive hour by hour in high school.

At the same time, in my other life I was being praised as "gifted." After the incredible vision at camp, the floodgates were open. I read for anyone, anytime. Friends and family asked me for tarot card readings—and if they didn't ask, I volunteered, sometimes even insisted. Have cards, will read—just try and stop me! I did readings for the Spanish club and the next-door neighbors. As a 15-year-old guru, I was soon invited to read at parties for my friends' parents. They loved me, and I craved the adulation.

Before I even got a driver's license, I was seeing things in the lives of the adults around me that other teenagers likely never thought about in connection with their own parents or their parents' friends. I saw affairs, abortions, miscarriages, children who didn't belong biologically to the fathers raising them, broken hearts—betrayals on so many levels that it made me dizzy to contemplate them. But I knew enough not to say exactly what I saw to people in their readings.

When I knew that a woman was having an affair, for example, I would say to her: "Why do I see two men in your heart?" If she wanted to talk about the affair, she would—and if she didn't, she would say the other man was her beloved father or brother or son. Reading for the unsuspecting husband a few minutes later was a little disconcerting. What did I say to him? "I sense

> I was seeing things other teenagers never thought about.
> I saw affairs, abortions, miscarriages, broken hearts—betrayals on so many levels that they made me dizzy.

you are feeling disconnected"—or something similarly benign. "Perhaps you should bring some more passion into the relationship," I would say. It's not easy giving sex advice when you're a virgin.

People always left my readings happy. In contrast, today they leave in a thoughtful or surprised, sometimes even angry, state. Six months, a year later, they will write to tell me how accurate the reading was— or how it changed their lives for the better. (Those are the best letters. I cherish them.) But my readings in high school were fun, entertaining, and not life changing. I was reading energy and seeing people's strengths—and perhaps a few weaknesses, which I downplayed. And many psychics do just that. They stay on the surface, never going deeper, and impress clients with their ability to explain what the colors of their auras say about them. I was, however, learning an important lesson as I skated on the surface of psychic work: what it feels like to have someone project their expectations upon me.

People who came to me for readings wanted me to fix things for them. (They still do!) And as a boy who yearned to be a superhero just so he could fix things for everybody, I tried to fulfill their expectations. I was giving advice on life experiences I'd certainly never had. They listened intently. What a role reversal! They were playing the part I was supposed to be playing at that stage of my life.

If only my mother had listened to me! My parents had realized that our nuclear family needed some major tweaking. That tweaking resulted in divorce, though both continued to live in Garden City. To increase my sense of a dual existence, I chose to live at both homes, switching houses every Sunday. My mother started a new romantic relationship—with Jorge, a homeless alcoholic, one of "the Guys." I have always been grateful that my mother is such an unconditionally loving person. But sometimes our good qualities can get us into trouble—as hers did then.

———◦———

I have always been grateful that my mother is such an unconditionally loving person. But sometimes our good qualities can get us into trouble.

———◦———

"This card says you should leave Jorge," I used to tell her, not because the card said anything of the sort but because I thought she should leave a dysfunctional (and painfully embarrassing to me) relationship. "And this card indicates that your choice is all wrong." Yeah—and the next card says you are going to buy me a new car. I was trying to manipulate her. True, I had good motives. Watching my mother with that man was one of the harder things in my life. Even as I write these words, I am afraid of what people will think of her. Who am I to judge my mother? We get along quite well now, but during my junior year in high school, we were practically strangers because of her love for this man.

❧ **I PLUNGED INTO ALL THINGS PSYCHIC.** Shopper's Village, a kind of cheesy indoor flea market, complete with a Pickle Alley and other such stores, suddenly held a special attraction for me: Stacy, the lisping psychic. Stacy had a little cubicle at the bottom of the escalator where she read cards for $10. I loved going to see her; I thought she was fabulous. I'd always stop by for a reading with Stacy, though none of my friends ever wanted to do it. Mind you, Stacy was a horrible psychic, though she would have made a great auctioneer. Her readings always began with the same spiel. She would shuffle the cards, then lay them out in rows of five.

"New moon, full moon, 2 weeksss' time, you will have your heartsss desssire, yesss?"

"Yes, what?"

"You have a lot of quessstionsss? You quessstion. It'sss your perssson to quessstion. Do you have any quessstionsss?" I had a lot of questions, like, How can you possibly make a living at this? But I liked the way she laid out the cards. She had big hair and long nails and was an actual, real practicing psychic.

Sometimes my mom and I would be driving down the street and I'd see a sign with a palm on it. "Mom, stop—I want to go in there!" And I'd run in and get a quick $10 reading. They were all awful. Not one of these people who ever read for me was even remotely talented, and I knew it, but I was intrigued by anyone who called themselves a psychic. I couldn't get enough.

On a visit to a New Age bookstore on Long Island, I spent a long time talking to the woman behind the counter. Ann had a feather in her hair, smelled like sage, and was wearing Birkenstocks. I was entranced.

Ann was a fairly well-known psychic on Long Island, very esoteric. She had the greatest accent, and her readings were all about sacred geometry and earth changes and how Miami would be the new Manhattan and someday California would fall off the earth. It was all quite strange and intense, but she was a loving woman; she comforted and hugged me, and I was very drawn to her. Ann was a channel (a person who allows a spirit to come into their body and speak through them) of Mother Mary. This was fascinating stuff.

An old wooden cabinet with shelves loaded down with crystals and stones stood in the small room where Ann did her readings. The entire time she read, you would hear movement from inside that cabinet. The sound of rattling and rocks shaking around was clearly audible. I have no idea what it was Ann actually did, but the energy was definitely moving in that room. When she laid her hands on you, they would get burning hot. Her predictions . . . well, I never bought any of them because they were so far-off. But that woman could move some energy. It was very cool. She never claimed to be a psychic. But she did some amazing work.

I wanted to learn everything I could from her. In order to see her on a regular basis, I lied to my dad and told him that I wanted to go into therapy again.

"Dad, there's this woman I think I should see."

"Fine. Now, she does have a degree?"

"Oh, sure, of course."

This was not such a big lie. Ann did have a degree, in art. Every week my dad would drive me to her house, thinking I was going to therapy, when in actuality I was getting a reading. I was more forthcoming with my mom; she actually came with me to Ann's to have a session. She remained very open about things like psychics and meditation, but despite her support, things were very rocky between us. Her love affair was a constant, ongoing source of misery.

During my sessions, I would sit down and just talk to Ann, so it really was therapy in a way.

"My parents are driving me crazy."

"Tell me more about that."

"My mother is in a fucked-up relationship, and my dad just drives me nuts."

"Dougall, don't judge your mother. We all have lessons to learn. She is a great teacher to you. Let's pray for her."

Ann would then have me lie down on her floor. She would light sage and begin to beat her drum from the corner of the room. As she moved into channel, I would stop listening to her words and focus on my mother. I could not help but cry.

Ann didn't try to predict things but worked with energy and breathing. She taught me how to manage my anger. Each week, I would discuss my life and what I was looking for. For sure, she wasn't terribly psychic—she used to tell me that she could see the woman I would end up with. Now, I can't blame that all on her. I was so terribly blocked. Denial can be incredibly strong. I was going home every night calling 970-COCK and loving it, but I was not ready to see it, or talk about it, or deal with it in any way, not even to myself.

I became addicted for a short time to gay sex lines. I told myself I was just "testing" to see if maybe there was something in that gay accusation after all. *Okay, I'll just see if these sex lines really turn me on. They probably won't . . . right?*

The voice at one sex line listed the options by saying: "If you want to talk to a woman, press one. If you want to talk to a live, hot man, press two." He certainly made that guy sound like a lot more fun than the woman. I pressed two. Remember, this was purely research. The live, hot man said, "Hello," and I had an orgasm almost immediately. Who knew that the word "hello" could be so compelling?

I called that sex line about 10 times a day. And I called a few others, too. When Mom found the bill, she asked if I was calling psychic hotlines. "Yes!" I said, eagerly jumping at this perfectly agreeable explanation. "I am testing them."

She said, "We can't afford any more tests."

Did *I* need any more tests?

Imagine my life: I was humiliated and reviled at high school—yet treated like a prophet by some of those kids' parents. Sometimes after school, I would go over to my friend Mark's house—his mother was a big fan of mine. She used to ask for readings all the time.

"Dougall, will you read for my friend?"

Mark's mother's girlfriend was over visiting this particular afternoon. I pulled my tarot cards from my backpack and sat down at the kitchen table.

"Pull three cards, please."

As I laid out the cards, I closed my eyes. In my head I could see a cartoon picture of a heart; inside of the heart was a large number two.

"Why do I see two people in your heart?"

"Excuse me?" Her jaw dropped. "Ummm, I've changed my mind—I don't want to do this." I found out later that night that she was having an affair on her husband.

TO MAKE MY LIFE MORE UNCOMFORTABLE, I KEPT TRYING TO PROVE I WAS STRAIGHT. Yes, I continued to spit and scratch—I even had a girlfriend for a while. The other boys still called me "fag." And most painful of all, I had the biggest crushes on a few of the guys who were the most cruel to me. Maybe they sensed I was hot for them and they were so repulsed, they spit venom at me. Now I wonder if it's possible one of them might have shared my feelings. Then, I would have sworn I was the only gay person in my entire school. And actually, to my knowledge, I am the only person from that class living an openly gay life to this day. I know others who still live in their closets. (Yes, boys, I have spotted you at gay bars. Come on out!)

But if there was a secret gay Mafia in my high school, I didn't know about it. Nobody ever whispered the password to me while I was fumbling to get the books out of my locker. Maybe the gay Mafia didn't want a fat kid in the club.

I increasingly looked outward for my validation, trying to escape. I became completely obsessed with all forms of meditation.

I meditated 2 hours a day and met with shamans, studied everything from *The Celestine Prophecy* to *Autobiography of a Yogi*. Ann owned a meditation center called the Higher Mind Center, which was basically her basement, where regular weekly meditation classes were held. Mom joined me for one of these classes as well. One of them was for Osho, or Bhagwhan Shree Rajneesh. He was a guru from India who was very popular in the 1980s. He started a big craze when he appeared on *60 Minutes*. He started everybody wearing orange, and rumors abounded about the orgies his followers had.

This was my first experience with people who followed a guru. It seemed like such a cool idea. I was told stories of this amazing man, who looked a lot like the Shah of Iran. I was told of his magical presence and the energy that he exuded from his eyes.

If there was a secret gay Mafia in my high school, I didn't know about it. Nobody ever whispered the password to me while I was fumbling to get the books out of my locker.

"Dougall, Osho is a great man," the meditation teacher told me reverently.

"What makes him so great?"

"He has found Buddha consciousness on this planet."

Every person in the room had a story as to how Osho had changed their life. I listened with great interest as they went around the room and spoke of their devotion to this guru. But something did not fit. *Follow him; he's so wonderful.* They all had that spacey, blissed-out look on their faces. His devotees all wore robes and something called a mala, a beaded necklace with Osho's picture on it. This was not for me. After hearing so many inspirational stories of this charming Indian man who had given up all worldly possessions, I was invited to watch a video of a lecture he once gave. The shot opened with an older Indian man pulling off the guru look quite well. I was a bit taken aback, as I had expected to see more of a Gandhi or starving Buddha look. What I actually saw was a man getting out of a Rolls-Royce, sporting quite a flashy Rolex. It was in that moment that I decided the whole guru thing was not my deal.

The moment I saw the guru getting out of a Rolls-Royce, sporting quite a flashy Rolex, I decided the whole guru thing was not my deal.

I did, however, learn from Osho. Until then, my experience with meditation had been quite basic. Osho taught all forms of meditation. He was the first person I'd heard of who talked about dancing or singing or laughing during meditation. He said that you didn't have to just stare at a candle and think. I thought his whole approach was very unique.

I came to Ann's meetings because I thought *all* of the approaches were interesting. I meditated while sitting, standing, dancing, and watching a strobe light. I was open to it all, and I certainly met the most unusual people. Everyone would show up to the meditations driving their cars plastered with New Age bumper stickers: *If the People Will Lead the Leaders Will Follow. Envision Whirled Peas. Lightworker.* Of course, they had crystals dangling from the rearview mirror. The other meditators were named Rainbow or had adopted new, Indian names. They were all really hippies. Looking back, I'm not sure if I was smelling sage or pot at these gatherings, but it didn't matter to me. I didn't know the difference.

There was a sweet German woman who would always hug me. But it wasn't just a regular hug—each and every time, it became a breathing contest of who could hold on longer. She would embrace me and suck all the air in, hold her breath, and then slowly let it out. Then the whole process would be repeated. I would be squirming by the end—*just let me go!* But this was classic New Age stuff. It was the whole spiritual thing of "I'm really taking your essence in. . . . Our genitals are touching, but it's not *that* kind of energy. . . . The energy between us is really flowing. . . ." Honestly, I was just like, *Get over yourself.* This touchy-feely stuff, I could do without.

Dad drove me to these meetings every week until I got my driver's license. Once I got my provisional license, I was free to do whatever I liked. I attended full-moon meditations, Osho meditations, even past-life regressions. I wanted so badly to see something—anything—during my past-life regression, but I drew a blank. Everyone else in the room had very intense experiences, but not me. The only thing I had was a very profound out-of-body experience. I totally left my body; I was floating on the ceiling. But I didn't have any visions; I saw nothing in terms of any past lives.

You name it, I came to it. Unless it had to do with exercise. Tai chi or karate—those I wasn't into. Anything involving exercise—forget it. But if it involved sitting and listening and staring, I was all for it. I became known as a very mystical kid. It goes without saying I was always the youngest person there by far, and I started to get a reputation as a young guru—the 15-year-old kid who "got it" and was enlightened at such an early age. I started getting asked how much I charged for a reading. These people expected to pay for my gift! It was a very strange life, having so much power with adults and so little with my peers. Most of my classmates were getting drunk and fooling around in back-

I attended full-moon meditations, Osho meditations, even past-life regressions. I wanted so badly to see something— anything. You name it; I came to it.

seats with girls; I was being spiritually hugged by a German woman.

After each meditation session, everyone always asked me what I saw. I would explain that I saw colors. From their reactions, I take it I was the only person who ever saw colors during meditation. I was honing my craft, but I was meditating far too much and ignoring every other aspect of my life. I was also spending way too much time in the company of adults. My parents were starting to become a bit concerned about my new friends.

"Lindsey said the funniest thing yesterday."

"Really, what class are you in with Lindsey?" my mother asked.

"Mom, Lindsey is a flight attendant! I know her from meditation!" Did she ever listen?

Ann nudged the owner of the bookstore where she worked to offer me a job, and I happily cut school to get to work on time. It didn't even seem like work, it was so fun. I read every book I could lay my hands on and soaked up all the people in the New Age community who gave me the respect and validation I was most certainly not getting from my peers.

I was so close to Ann and the rest of the meditation group that I joined them on a spiritual vision quest to Sedona, Arizona, during my junior year of high school. Sedona is renowned as a spiritual place and a powerful energy center. Some of the oldest exposed rocks on earth are located there, in stunning, dramatic 1,000-foot-tall forma-

tions. Centuries ago, Native Americans gathered to perform cere-
monies in the sacred Red Rocks. Naturally it draws all sorts of psychics
and healers and shamans.

Sedona was the ideal destination for my new crowd. Our group
consisted of 20 mature women, all between the ages of 40 and 60,
each wearing her dream-catcher bag and clutching crystals. And me.

And it was fantastic. When we left the airport, we all got into a
van and drove down the stark desert highway. For miles and miles
there was nothing to see, just desert. Then we went around a bend,
and all of a sudden the most spectacular, otherworldly rock formations appeared all around us, dwarfing the highway and our van. It
was really amazing. It was the kind of landscape that had me instantly
imagining that some hot young Native American brave in a headdress
would swoop by on his horse, carry me away, and make me his slave.

That didn't happen. I was still "Dances with No One."

We drove into Sedona proper and wandered the quaint village,
which was surrounded by more incredible rock formations. Suddenly,
we turned a corner and were in a New Age mini-mall. Shop after shop
of herbal water and dream catchers and crystals and beads and silver.
So much for reaching into the ethers—I needed to shop!

At one main street in Sedona, if you stand on a certain corner
and look to your right, you'll see the most beautiful, breathtaking natural vista; look to your left, and you see a swap meet. It was a jarring
meeting of the spiritual and the commercial.

On our first day, we all rose with the sun and gathered in a circle
on the sacred rocks. The trip was being sponsored by a woman healer,
Tamara, but everyone from our meditation class went as a group.
Every woman in the circle wore hiking boots, sunglasses, a bag filled
with crystals around her neck—the whole thing. We all had to go
around the circle and introduce ourselves.

Tamara, our leader, had decided that we would all sing our names to one another. This was more of the kind of New Age crap I just couldn't get into. Tamara started. It worked this way: "My name is . . ." in her normal voice. Then . . . "T-a-a-a-a-m-a-a-a-a-r-a-a-a," going up and down the scale for at least 10 seconds. We all were to then sing her name back to her in the same way. I was next . . . and I literally just mumbled, "Do-gull." It was all I could bring myself to do. I had shifted the tone, and our leader was not amused. Fine. I just passed the talking stick on to the next woman and had a laughing fit. After that, the singing circle didn't really go as Tamara had planned.

But the rest of the trip was so much fun. We went to all the places that were supposedly sacred and did all kinds of meditations and the medicine wheel and everything. There were a lot of Native American guides that week, for sure. I shopped like a madman. I still have the Native American rattle I bought, and the peace pipe, too. The rattle cost about $100, which was a lot of money at the time, but I was charging wildly to my dad's credit card, so I didn't care. I brought the rattle to the circle and was so excited, and Ann, my mentor, solemnly told me to play it with joy. To think that most kids my age were in Daytona Beach for spring break, dousing themselves in liquor, and I was atop a red mountain, trying to figure out my totem animal.

Of course, I gave readings to my fellow travelers, and one of the women said to me, "You know, I love Ann. She's wonderful and spiritual. But you've got a real gift. It is just amazing, the things you knew about me." It was very weird to be told that I was better than the woman I considered my guru. I felt a little tension about it, though she was always very supportive. Ann was everything to me. In retrospect, I can see that she was the mother my own mother wouldn't, or couldn't, be for me that year.

I started to really believe that I had a true gift for reading. People on the trip to Sedona were astounded by my accuracy. Imagine: You're a 50-year-old woman going on a trip with your girlfriends, and a 15-year-old boy is there? Not to mention, the 15-year-old knocks you out with a reading, telling you things he couldn't possibly have any way of knowing? The women on my trip were all extremely encouraging. They'd smile and tell one another proudly, "He's so evolved."

To think that most kids my age were in Daytona Beach for spring break, dousing themselves in liquor, and I was atop a red mountain, trying to figure out my totem animal.

⬤ THIS EVOLUTION WAS ALL TOO MUCH FOR MY SUBURBAN CLASSMATES, and the torture at school continued. Admittedly, I was over-the-top with this stuff; it was all I talked about. My math teacher told me, "If you spent as much time studying geometry as you do the tarot cards, you'd do really well." What was I ever going to do with geometry?

I preferred to spend my time in study hall designing my own business cards. They'd have three tarot cards on the right, a little wizard on the left, and the words "Dougall Fraser, Psychic" in the middle. I spent a great deal of time getting every detail on those business cards just right. I also came up with pricing charts, debating endlessly how much I would charge and how it should all work, but never really thinking it was possible. I couldn't see how I could really fit my passion into a real life. I wasn't going to be Stacy, the lisping psychic at

the mall. I didn't want to do what Ann was doing, channeling, because there seemed to be something quite weird about it. No, I wasn't
so sure about the channeling.

> I couldn't understand how sitting in a sweaty, dirty tepee for 4 hours would get me more spiritual.

As much as I enjoyed everything I was doing, I did not want to sing my name in a circle. There was still a large part of me that did not gravitate toward the more "airy" parts of the New Age world. I didn't want to wear a dream catcher on my head. In Sedona, for example, I hadn't wanted to go to the sweat lodge. I couldn't understand how sitting in a sweaty, dirty tepee for 4 hours would get me more spiritual. That had caused a stir in the group, but I just couldn't see the point. I thought that to be a psychic, I had to buy into all that, grow long hair and use crystal deodorant and have vitamin breath. I was just me, and I couldn't see my path. I hadn't seen anyone I could identify as a normal, successful person who happened to work as a psychic for a living. That's why every time Ann would say to me, "You really should become a psychic," I'd think, *No way.*

I was very content to be her little helper. After the meditation session with the regulars who came every week, Ann would channel for the group. That meant that for 45 minutes, Ann would bring a spirit through her and go on about how the earth was going to hell, pretty much. Every time Ann finished her channeling, she would fall over in a dead faint. She'd be sitting there with her eyes closed, talking—"It is so wonderful to be here with all of you during this time . . ."—when *bam.* She'd fall on the floor every time. I mean, just keel over and hit the ground. You knew the session was at an end when she fell down.

As Ann became more popular, I would follow her to her events with a pillow in tow. It was my job to catch her, or at the very least position pillows so she wouldn't hurt herself when she fell. There was one event with at least 75 to 100 people in attendance, and Ann walked around the whole time with her eyes closed. I knew she was going to go down any minute when she got to "A new lifting . . . a new day . . ." and I was frantically chasing her with pillows. (I've been doing readings for 10 years now and have never yet fallen over from reading for someone.) After the fall, Ann would slowly sit up and return to us, murmuring, "That was wonderful." It was hysterical, the drama connected with all this! It was too much.

This all sounds a bit harsh, and it isn't meant to be. I loved Ann, worshipped her, and was eagerly studying everything she opened my mind to. I was a true believer. But we in the New Age community all have our little quirks. Hers happened to be falling over. I had read somewhere that burping means that energy is coming through you, so I used to make it a point to burp during sessions. I also used to shake because I thought that if energy was moving through my body, I should shake. I was feeling my way, learning, deciding what did and did not work for me in this whole new world.

There is a very famous channel named Jane Roberts, who while she was channeling would smoke a cigarette and drink a beer. She claimed that was what Seth, the entity who supposedly came through her, wanted. To that I can only say, "Come on, Jane. Lighten up and have a smoke!" Supposedly Jane never touches cigarettes—only when Seth is present because it's he who wants these things. If that's the case, then I do channel—a spirit who only wants Gucci shoes. I only buy them when Sven is in my body. Sure!

Chapter Five

WHO LEAVES NEW YORK
TO BE FREE?

HIGH SCHOOL HAD BECOME INTOLERABLE TO ME, the guru, by age 16. I hated being powerless and taunted at school when I commanded so much attention and respect outside the classroom. I was old enough to drop out on my own, but I knew I couldn't support myself yet as a psychic. Nor did I have any conviction that I could make a living and have any semblance of a normal life without veering off into the path of channeling or lisping at a booth at Shopper's Village.

So I devised a plan, one that depended on my divorced parents not communicating too closely with each other. They didn't. I told Dad that Mom was dating a homeless alcoholic who spent a lot of time at our house—she was, he did—and I wanted out. And I told Mom that Dad and I couldn't really talk and that I needed to move. I also told her point-blank, "I refuse to stay here if you are going to continue that relationship." Deep down inside, I thought if I threatened to leave for real, my mom would break off the romance. But she didn't.

"Obviously I can't live with either parent," I said reasonably. "I'm miserable in high school. I want to move to Dallas to be closer to

Tarrin"—who had graduated from college, had moved to Texas, and was working as a massage therapist—"but I want my own apartment."

I was stunned when they agreed to everything I asked. With a minimum of contact between them, my parents worked out an arrangement where they would give me $800 a month, plus pay my car insurance. A nice Dallas apartment cost $350. This was not a bad deal. Their only requirement was that I earn my GED and be enrolled in some kind of school by September.

Naturally this was not a popular decision among my extended family. Relatives on both sides criticized my parents for supporting this move. But my dad had some sympathy for my position. He remembered chafing under the expectations of his parents and being afraid to follow his dream career. Clearly school wasn't happening for me, nor did I have any interest in learning his business. My mom wasn't about to budge on the matter of Jorge. Dad felt that it was the right answer at the time. In the end, both my parents were being as supportive as they could be, faced with a kid who had dropped out after 11th grade. They believed in my talent and thought I had a great hobby, but I'm sure they thought someday I would have to find a real job.

I left Garden City 2 days after the last day of 11th grade. I only told my closest friends. I did not tell any of my teachers for fear that some corny after-school-special intervention would take place. (Obviously I had seen plenty of Lifetime movies.) In less than a week, I had my own apartment in Dallas and I was facing the Texas Educational Board.

Like a good double agent, I played my cards right to the end. My last mission was acquiring the almighty GED. There was a slight problem. I'd put so much effort into espionage in high school that I hadn't retained much information on the major subjects—like, you know, English, math, and science. The state of Texas, surprisingly enough, did not have chakras on the exam or the history of numerology as one of the essay questions. And the first question, before I got to the actual test, was "When did you drop out?"

"I haven't," I told the woman in charge, thinking she would be impressed by my ambition in going for my GED before I'd even missed a semester of school.

"What do you mean you haven't dropped out?" she demanded.

"I'm on summer break," I said.

"You have to drop out."

"But I am not a dropout. I just want to graduate early."

"*You must drop out*," she insisted.

"May I use your phone?" I asked. "Yes, Operator, Garden City, New York. Garden City High School." When a receptionist answered, I said, "Hi, this is Dougall Fraser. I am dropping out." This satisfied the Texas GED administrator, and I was allowed to take the test.

> **The state of Texas, surprisingly enough, did not have chakras on the GED exam or the history of numerology as one of the essay questions.**

My goal was to become a great healer, and my parents had insisted that I enroll in some kind of school, so I settled on massage as the quickest and most direct route to actually getting my hands on people and helping them. I had vague visions of eventually becoming an acupuncturist or an herbalist or some kind of healer. Massage school was just the route I chose.

I was really scared when I had to go for my interview. Most massage schools accept students automatically—you hand over your money, and you're a student. It's not like you need good SAT scores to get in. But because massage deals with naked people, the law requires that students be 18 years of age or older. I was only 17 and hadn't received the results of my GED test yet, but I fibbed and said I had already gotten it. The director and I figured out that by the time the 6-month program was over, I would have turned 18, so I could enroll on a technicality.

The school was unique in a variety of ways. Aesthetically it wasn't a palace — the Whole Body Concepts School of Massage took up the corner space of a small one-story office building. When I entered, I got the feeling that I might have stepped into a cult. Bright-eyed Southerners, all wearing white, greeted me with warm but slightly puzzled smiles. *What's this kid doing here?*

I'd had my interview with Sam, the director of the massage school, and the whole time, I couldn't figure out if Sam was a man or a woman. I still didn't know when I left. When I arrived at school for the first day, the director was now called Samantha. My interview had obviously taken place during his transition period from male to female. This was a far cry from Garden City High. We'd had our special teachers, but a transsexual was indeed a first. Not that I was judging; in fact, for me it was quite a humbling experience. I realized quickly that I was now to deal with adult issues. I respected Samantha. She was caring, listened to me, and most importantly, let me call her by her first name.

Classes were tougher than I expected them to be. Students were expected to learn about muscles, the skeletal system, human biology. . . . I didn't give a rat's ass about any of that stuff. There are two kinds of massage students: One is the kind who acts almost as if they're becoming surgeons. They take it all very seriously, like they're going to med school. I was the exact opposite kind of student. I was not there because I really cared about fixing carpal tunnel syndrome. I was there because I wanted to be a Modern Medicine Man, and massage seemed like the appropriate business move. School was only a 6-month course. After graduation, I would have an instant career; plus, it would give me license to start some kind of spiritual healing practice. Not to mention I was thinking, *Hey, I get to wear sweatpants!* I was coming in late every day; I was totally chilling. Basically, I looked at massage school as going to a spa for 6 months.

🍃 CLASSES WERE HELD MONDAY THROUGH FRIDAY. One day was theory, where we had lectures and learned about the physical body, and the next day was massage. It went back and forth — one day lecture, next day massage, next day lecture, next day massage. There were all kinds of people in my class, ranging from 20-somethings to women in their forties searching for a career to wealthy people who thought it would be a kick to become massage therapists. Some were very into all things New Age, some were not; but I was immediately and definitely pegged as the New Age guy. I talked all the time about energy work and healing and someday opening up a holistic center. The students all got to know one another well, really quickly, because we were all naked by the second day of class.

It was very nerve-racking for a virgin to be naked in front of 20 strangers–though, of course, I denied the whole virgin thing. *Oh, yeah, all girls all the time — that's me.* They weren't falling for it. Disrobing was painful. I was still overweight, with plenty of body issues of my own. The very first lesson we learned was how to tie a toga. We all headed for the bathrooms, undressed completely, and tied two sheets around ourselves in makeshift togas. The sheet origami was horrid. I stood in the bathroom, wrapping a twin sheet around my soft, pudgy 6'6" frame with the thought of my peers, left back in Garden City, swimming in my head. I looked in the mirror and realized everything had changed. I was naked, living in Dallas, Texas. I was about to walk into a room full of strangers. Mothers, transsexuals, athletes, a dentist, divorcées, gay, straight—and then me, high school dropout.

Most people go to their first toga party at a fraternity. Mine was at a massage school.

"Dougall, you can do this."

I focused on my breath. In my mind's eye, I begin to swirl pink light around my body. (Pink is the color of unconditional love.) I accepted my body as much as I could in that moment. As the light merged with my physical body, my angst diminished significantly. As I opened my eyes again, somehow the face staring back at me in the mirror was older, wiser, and adult. Off I went.

We all emerged, wearing our togas, and entered the classroom that held about 30 massage tables. Half the class lay on the table (the "body"), while the other half prepared to give them massages.

The next lesson was draping: covering the body of the person being massaged to expose only the part being worked on. This was all about learning to fold the sheet and tuck it to expose just a leg, then just an arm, and so on. It was important to know how to keep the genitals and women's breasts covered. There were plenty of mistakes the first week in draping. You learn very quickly in massage never to say, "Whoops." People usually don't realize that they've been exposed, so if you're calm about it and ignore it, they don't get insecure.

At the start of massage school, each student was supposed to go out and buy two sets of sheets, which we brought with us each day to school to work on. I went to the store and must have bought 40 different sheets. I was a lunatic about my table. It had to have extra foam, a special cover. . . . God forbid I would crack open the anatomy book or the physiology book, but my table sure looked good. My towels always matched the sheets. I had more sheets than anyone else in the class and I was proud of it. (Meanwhile, of course, I was still telling myself, *I'm not gay. I just have a thing for sheets.*)

There were quite a few gay students in the school. In fact, it was mostly run by gays and lesbians. It wasn't as bad as high school—they didn't outright attack me—but they were all certainly aware of the fact that I was gay and discussed it among themselves. Actually it was quite sweet, looking back. I remember Samantha asking me point-blank if I was gay. It wasn't meant badly—it was more like "You're gay, right?"—but at the time it seemed like such a horrible moment. These were my peers, obviously socially advanced, and not all of them were falling for my guru dance.

You learn very quickly in massage never to say, "Whoops."

I decided to take matters into my own hands. I called everyone together and said, "It's ridiculous that you all are always talking about me! I'm not gay. . . . I'm just comfortable with my sexuality!" It was painful. They all just looked at me. *Right, sure, whatever you say.* I raised holy hell, which of course only made me seem gayer.

WE STARTED WITH THE BASICS. I learned all the strokes—effleurage, petrissage, tapotement. It was a lot to learn, but all the practice time gave us a chance to develop our own particular styles. Are you deep, are you light, what makes people tickle, what does a muscle feel like, which areas are you supposed to concentrate on? That part was fun. I got a 2-hour massage every other day and spent the rest of my time gossiping with my friends. That was my experience of massage school, as I skipped the studying part.

Massage school introduced me to my body. The sensuality of it. Not sexuality, but the magic of the human form. I am truly amazed at these "machines" that our souls dwell in. I was not an athlete. I did not work out. I was not experimenting with girls—or boys, for that matter—and had some body issues stemming from sexual abuse. In massage school, I learned about my body, and I learned to love it.

I searched for another job at a New Age bookstore at night. Above and Beyond was your classic New Age bookstore that stocked books, crystals, capes, jewelry, tarot cards, and so on. Once a month, they hosted a psychic fair. I tried long and hard to get a job there, when, frankly, they really should have hired me immediately. I was the perfect employee for a New Age bookstore. I had experience, after all; plus, I read all the new titles and knew what each and every crystal was for. If a customer came in looking for the *I Ching*, I had read three and could lead her right to them. If a woman wanted to buy a crystal to bring more love into her life, I knew that rose quartz was the way to go. I was great at the sales part, but I really had to talk them into hiring me.

I was so young and not particularly well-educated, but finally I convinced them. (Do not try this at home, folks.)

> I learned about my body, and I learned to love it. I am truly amazed at these "machines" that our souls dwell in.

"Hi, my name is Dougall Fraser, and I know that I am going to work here."

"Pardon me?"

"Let me repeat myself. I'm Dougall Fraser, quite psychic, if I do say so myself, and I am going to work here!"

There seemed to be some concern about my age, but I did a great job of just not telling them. I never even filled out an application. I talked about my apartment and my car and the fact that I lived alone, and I think they just assumed I was at least 21. Not 17. Because your average 17-year-old was in study hall, or at the mall, or doing whatever the hell "normal" kids do.

Above and Beyond had both a massage therapist and a regular psychic in the back of the store. The psychic's name was Kristen, and I personally thought she was awful, but she had a big following in Dallas. She had such a great story—Kristen had actually inherited her tarot cards from her grandmother! I thought that was just in the movies. She came from a long line of fortune-tellers.

Part of my job was booking Kristen's appointments. She had some charming clients. They would call in tears.

"I just saw Kristen yesterday. I need to talk with her immediately."

"I'm sorry. Kristen is in session."

"Well, I need her now. My boyfriend hasn't called, and Kristen told me to duct-tape my telephone to the ceiling so I would not call him. I need to know when I can take my phone off the ceiling!"

"Are you serious?"

"*Would I be kidding?! I need to talk to my psychic right now!*"

"I will give her the message."

Kid you not.

The bookstore was owned by a couple who battled all the time. They were hardly the most spiritual people. When I started working there, they were dating, but they eventually called the romance off and just worked together. They had really bad fights. Once, he threw a chair at her. Staff meetings were always awful. The atmosphere was poisonous. As the cashier, I was always amused when customers would come in and comment on how clear the energy was. It was so not clear in there!

Even I was guilty of misjudging the store. Before I worked there, I was positive that the owners were just a phone call away from God. I was sure anyone who actually owned a bookstore dedicated to the occult must have amazing psychic potential. Once I was on the other side of the counter, I realized that the business aspect of contacting the "other side" came with all the same politics any company had. Staff meetings did not involve chanting or herbal remedies. It was a business like any other. Filled with gossip, drama, deception, and of course petty office politics. But they did have the best psychic fair around!

> **I realized the business of contacting the "other side" came with all the same office politics.**

Above and Beyond held its psychic fair on the first Sunday of every month. We hosted 18 to 20 psychics, each set up at their own card table in one of two classrooms. It was my job to manage the schedule, which was drawn up on a chalkboard in a big grid. One side of the grid had the whole day broken into 15-minute increments, while the other listed each psychic's name. The idea was to fill up the whole board so each psychic was fully booked. Since I was the cashier, each customer came in and bought a ticket from me; then we looked at the board together. I'd say something like, "Well, Dory is available at 12:15. She's an astrologer. It will be fun—you'll get a chart" or "LeeAnne is available at 12:30, and she will read the cards and make some predictions for you." The good psychics did 24 readings back-to-back without a break. They were popular, and all their time slots filled up quickly.

I wanted so badly to have my own card table and give readings, but I wasn't allowed to. I wasn't considered a psychic. I was a kid in massage school. I worshipped the other psychics who came in once a month—I thought they were just great. I'd study them and wonder how they could do their work with so many people around. The fairs were really intense; it was like watching psychic boot camp. I had been giving casual readings for years, ever since Camp Dudley, but it was just a hobby, for fun. I certainly didn't charge money. Occasionally when a woman would come in and say, "I really need a book right now," I'd answer, "You need a book because you don't have a job, right?" She'd be shocked and say, "How did you know that?" I'd just say, "Oh, I feel it around you, so here's a good book for you." The manager would be really surprised and ask how I'd come up with that, since I didn't have tarot cards or anything. I just kind of did it. I was practicing.

On the average day, instead of stacking and shelving books, I'd be reading about healing and Reiki, gathering all the free knowledge I could get. As time went on, occasionally when I got really bored, I read customers' cards for free. I didn't know what the cards meant—though I'd owned my own deck since the age of 9, I'd never studied them in depth. But I'd come up with things like "Your partner just cheated on you," and no one ever guessed it wasn't coming from the cards.

I might get $20 here and there, or someone might come to my house for a reading every other week or so, but that was the extent of it. If it was my night to close at the shop, I would ask any remaining customers if they would like a free reading.

One night, I approached a young woman who was browsing through the books. "Miss, would you like a free psychic reading before you leave?"

She looked me up and down like I was another heap of metal on a used car lot. She hesitated for a moment but decided to take me up on my offer.

"May I hold your hand?"

"Yes."

"What is your name?"

"My name is Rebecca."

As Rebecca said her name, I closed my eyes. I focused just on the sound of her voice. In my mind's eye, I could see a little girl around the age of 5.

"You have a daughter."

"Yes! I do!"

"This may not make any sense to you. But that relationship was not a mistake. Your daughter needed to be born; he was just the vessel."

When I opened my eyes, Rebecca was leaning in toward me. She was too close.

"Would you like to have dinner sometime?"

"Um. No thank you."

I was watching and learning and practicing. I was good at making predictions; it came easily to me, and I still liked that I could impress people with this skill. My ability made me feel special. Superhuman.

EACH TIME WE HELD A FAIR, MYSTERIOUSLY ENOUGH, THE BETTER PSYCHICS SEEMED TO BE IN THE BIGGER ROOM. When I would say, "Megan is available at 2," the customer would immediately ask, "Is she in the smaller classroom?" If I answered yes, she'd say, "I don't want to go to someone in the small room." They created a hierarchy that didn't even exist!

One month, I decided to shake things up. I knew I could put Leslie and her card table in a gutter and she would still book 24 readings; she was that popular. I also knew she wouldn't care, so I put her in the small room, along with some others, and really mixed things up. The psychics freaked out. One came up to me, an older woman with crystals hanging from her hair, saying, "I can't read in that room! It doesn't face east!" Leslie knew it didn't matter where she was, but Linda had to have her clients sitting to her left. John liked being in his own room. Those who went from the large classroom to the small classroom thought they had been demoted. Those who were now in the large classroom had smiles on their faces and probably gave better readings because they believed we had promoted them.

It was ridiculous. Just by switching rooms, I had created utter chaos. The clients were confused, saying, "My psychic's no longer any good. She's in the small room!" All I was trying to do was impart a very small lesson: The classroom doesn't matter.

I thought it was funny, but I can't say it went over very well. Hundreds of people had a collective, complete meltdown. It was soon afterward that I was fired from Above and Beyond.

Observing those psychic fairs was my first real experience of seeing and hearing intentional bullshit from other psychics. (Stacy from Long Island was just as bad, but at least she meant well.) At Above and Beyond, one psychic carried a pendulum around with her everywhere. She literally could not make a move without consulting it. She'd say things like "Universe, am I supposed to have a steak?" If the pendulum swung one way, she'd announce triumphantly, "The universe wants me to have a steak!" I'd sit there thinking, *Get a life! Eat a steak, don't eat a steak, but get over yourself.* Or at the end of the fair, they'd all complain about how drained they were, how they just couldn't keep doing it, that it was so exhausting. I thought it was all crap. Sage had to be burned, this crystal had to be facing east—all of these little rituals had to be observed. This little clique of people, with this constant underlying battle of "who's better than who."

Observing those psychic fairs was my first real experience of seeing intentional BS from other psychics.

I just couldn't take any of that stuff seriously. Well, that's not fair. Their idiosyncrasies just bugged me. Mine, of course, were all normal. I was still burping to show the energy moving through my body. The louder and deeper the burp, the more on target I must have been. So Peggy had her pendulum, Brenda had her rattle, and I had my burping.

❡ BACK AT SCHOOL, I LEARNED TO GIVE A REALLY PROFESSIONAL MASSAGE. I was good at giving a relaxing massage. It was not therapeutic—if you had gotten into a car accident and needed therapy, I wasn't the best one to help, but I was very good at calming and soothing people seeking stress relief.

Even though I was a good masseur, my grades were pretty bad. Here I was, finally doing what I thought I wanted to do, and still my grades were bad. The book learning, the lectures on anatomy, the technical stuff—I hated it. I was interested in the business end, in learning how to set up and run a massage business; but contraindications, and sprained tendons, and stretching . . . I couldn't have cared less.

There's more work involved in becoming a masseur than many people think. Texas law required 700 hours of work before you could become certified; New York required 1,000. At the end of the 6-month course, I had to complete an internship, which basically meant I had to work for free for the school. I had to give 50 free 1-hour massages before I could graduate.

I had pretty much coasted through the 6 months and still graduated and gotten certified. I didn't know anything about the physical body, but I knew how to relax a client. Many students took it all much more seriously; they liked helping people heal from injuries. That wasn't my deal. I wanted candles and ocean music in the background.

I thought the whole thing was going to be fun, though there were a couple of small omens that it might not all be smooth sailing. During my internship, for example, one woman asked if I would lick chocolate sauce off her body. It was my first warning that a masseur might not necessarily be treated that well.

Most of my fellow graduates headed to Whole Foods to do chair massage or got a job at a chiropractor's office. I had a whole practice fall into my lap. A woman had contacted the school because she and her husband were moving to Oregon and she wanted to sell her practice. Tarrin and I went to meet Kendra and fell in love with her. She was really cool and nice, a hard worker, and she loved her clients. She was looking for the right people to sell her practice to and make a small profit. For our money, we would get an office with two therapy rooms, a waiting room, and an established client base.

It was an incredible opportunity for my sister and me. We bought the practice immediately—we only needed to come up with about $5,000 cash. Kendra had probably done five to seven clients a day, so Tarrin and I split her workload and did very well. My father was very supportive of our new business. His main suggestion was that we wear uniforms. Many people in the massage community go the medical route—surgical mask, the whole bit—or they do what Tarrin and I did, which was wear jeans and shirts. We preferred that kind of casual environment.

The first big sign that I was not cut out for a life of massage was the overwhelming amount of laundry that came with the practice. You cannot imagine how many sheets and towels a masseur goes through in a workday. According to Texas state law, I was supposed to change the sheets before every new client came in. Now, I didn't have a washer and dryer at home. I wasn't about to change the sheets four times a day. My personal philosophy was if you got on my table and I wasn't grossed out by you—if I myself would lie on the sheets after you left—then I would just leave them there. (I remember some of my clients saying to me, "Dougall, these sheets feel a little damp. . . .")

I soon grew to hate doing massage. It was so boring! I'm a talker, and when someone comes for a massage, they're looking for a break, for restful silence. They want to hear New Age music or a brook babbling in the background. I didn't want to do that. If the client talked to me, they would get a much better massage. We could gab while I worked on them and have a good time together.

The first big sign that I was not cut out for a life of massage was the overwhelming amount of laundry that came with the practice.

I had one client whom I adored. I could relate to her in many ways—she had body-image and weight issues. I would always give her an hour and a half, 30 minutes above the normal duration of a session, because I just loved her. We would talk—it was like therapy—and I would also give her readings. Her late father had been a palm reader/numerologist, and I could actually feel his energy in sessions and pass on messages. There were moments she would be on the table in tears. Eventually she decided to take the money she was investing in massage and hire a trainer, and we both cried because we weren't going to see each other anymore. That was a very special relationship—but these relationships were few and far between.

Many of our clients were rich Dallas socialites who treated us poorly. Understand, though, they were under tremendous stress about redecorating. Seriously, redoing their curtains was a big ordeal to them, so they came to their massage therapists after curtain selection.

I got tired of it in a hurry. I was working on these tiny, little socialites who had thighs the size of my index finger. I was supposed to massage *that* for 10 minutes? Please, get over yourself. I did not care for their attitude, and my own attitude toward my work took a nosedive. My massage clients started leaving in droves, and I couldn't blame them because I wasn't really giving them what they deserved. If they paid for a full hour, it was just torturous to me. I was bored out of my mind after the first 15 minutes. I was only doing about 10 massages a week, and even that number started to dwindle. By this time, Tarrin was living with her boyfriend and had a whole life with him, so she was happy with a light workload.

I started to do a few readings here and there. I would move the massage table to the other side of the room, set up a card table, cover it with my star-and-moon tablecloth, and spread out my cards. But this was still pretty sporadic. I did many more massages than readings.

That first year I had my own business was such a painful part of my life. I was eating constantly. I weighed close to 300 pounds, though I don't know the exact number because I had gotten so big that I refused to weigh myself. I was so insecure. I was a virgin, I wasn't dating, and I was still in the closet. I went to work, giving massages I hated doing, then went home and read spiritual books and ate. I was battling with my sexuality and my identity in general. I knew I had this great ability, but I wasn't using it. Sure, I did parlor tricks to impress people, but that was all. I tried to make it look good; I could tell people things that would astound them, so I tried to keep up the image of someone who was very spiritual, who went home each night to meditate. I was really going home to eat Chinese.

I would do things like order two sodas so the restaurant would think I was ordering for more than one person. If Tarrin happened to be visiting, I'd make her answer the door so the delivery guy would think more than one person lived there. Once I bounced a check and

> **The universe wasn't going to reward me until I started to take care of myself.**

went through the register, trying to figure it out. Who, I wondered, was Panda? It appeared over and over in the ledger: Panda. Panda. Panda. I suddenly realized it was my local Chinese restaurant. It was bad.

I was also a slob. I never cleaned my closets. If you were to open the closet in my bedroom, hundreds of things would come tumbling out. As I look back, it's not hard to get the symbolism: I was in the closet, searching for my identity. I was struggling to become what I thought I could be. But I was learning a life lesson that I now often try to explain to my clients: The universe wasn't going to reward me until I started to take care of myself.

Chapter Six

COMING OUT

MY LIFE LOOKED MORE OR LESS OKAY ON THE OUTSIDE. I was holding it together, but just barely. I was earning just a little less than it took to survive from my massage business and part-time psychic work. I didn't have much of a social life. All I did was work, hole up in my apartment, and eat constantly. I knew I had a unique talent, but had no idea of how to translate my gift into a career.

My massage business was slowly going down; I continued to lose clients and not really even care. I was tired of the whole thing. I was sick of the occasional late-night calls from potential male clients who called and said something like, "You look like a nice young boy. I sure do like to *release*." I suppose that was my fault. I had created a flyer that offered an "hour of peace." My tagline was that I offered "holistic bodywork in a safe environment for people to rest, relax, and release." My little virgin mind had no idea what some people thought of as a release. My voice mail messages were frequently quite vile. And my regulars were tired of my lackluster massage.

Without my business, I had nothing except food for comfort. Everything seemed to be going in a slow downward spiral. I was not living much of a life at age 19.

It was a humid Dallas night in July when I went to meditation class, the same one I'd been attending for more than a year. I was feeling extremely vulnerable. Each week the teacher, the other two students, and I meditated on a specific color; then we'd all come back and talk about how that color had affected us. This particular week our chosen color was blue, the color of truth and fear. During the "blue" week, it was common to face one's fears. We concentrated on being as authentic as possible.

The meditation teacher had left the door to the room open a couple of inches, instead of closing it like she usually did. The crack of light was really bothering me; it was all I could focus on. When it was my turn to share, the first thing I said was, "I'd like you to close the door."

She heard something in my voice. "All right, Dougall."

She closed the door, and everyone looked at me expectantly. I put my head down and took a deep breath. "There's something I'd like to say, but I'm really, really scared."

There was dead silence in the room. Tears welled up in my eyes and I could barely choke out, "Lately I've been questioning . . . my sexuality." I burst into tears the moment those words left my mouth. You could have heard a pin drop in that room. My announcement was greeted with utter silence. No one had any idea of what to say—because, of course, they already had more than an inkling that I was gay!

The effect of saying those words, after a lifetime of repressing them and the feelings behind them, was incredibly liberating.

The effect of saying those words, after a lifetime of repressing them and the feelings behind them, was incredibly liberating. After I managed to say those six little words to other people out loud, I instantly felt free. I felt so much better, in fact, that within 10 minutes I had moved past the questioning stage and announced flat-out, "I'm gay. I'm not questioning it; I know it." The four of us talked for hours, late into the night, about my fears of being authentic and my new sense of discovery. The truth was certainly being told during that particular meditation class. In that moment, I was focusing on the fact that I was homosexual, but the real lesson was to learn to be genuine about my entire identity. And the truth did set me free.

I drove home to my apartment in my turquoise Jetta, which was just another symbol. I remembered the day I bought the car. When I got in and drove off the lot, I actually thought, *This is a faggot's car*, even as I swore to myself I was not gay. I had to laugh when I thought about it. The relief I felt was tremendous. I called my sister the second I got in the door at midnight and told her she had to come over immediately because I had something important to tell her.

She arrived in 10 minutes. (She later told me she had known what I was going to say.) She seated herself on the couch and looked at me expectantly. I sat in a chair facing her and told her, "Tarrin, I'm gay."

She burst into tears and jumped up to hug me. "I know," she said, which was not the response I was looking for.

"Don't say that!" How deflating. This was a major revelation! She could have at least humored me a little. All this time, I'd been giving what I considered to be an Oscar-worthy performance of the young hetero guy.

"Do you think Mom knows?" I asked anxiously.

"Dougall, everyone knows—we were just wondering if you did!"

Of course, the next thing I said was, "Do you want something to eat?" So I made us some food and we sat up really late, talking things over.

The very next morning, I called my mother. When she answered the phone, I said, "Mom, are you busy?"

She told me no, so I said, "I'm gay."

She replied, "I know." This was getting quite annoying. Here I'd just had a profound, life-changing breakthrough, and all anyone had to say was, "I know, I know, I know." We laughed, and then we cried, and Mother, as always, was completely accepting and loving. I still didn't want my father to know at this point, or Tarrin's fiancé. I had it in my mind that I wasn't going to tell them until after I'd had sex— until I'd sealed the deal, as it were. It was enough for me at the moment that my mom and sister knew. I wanted to take some time and get used to the whole idea.

For the first time as an adult, I decided that I wanted to go to therapy and work on coming out of the closet. I'd been taking care of my spiritual body for years, doing all kinds of meditation and healing work. But a lot of my spiritual quest was avoiding this world. I read books on ascension and spent far too much time alone, meditating. I needed to have a social life. I knew it would be hard to find the right therapist because I'd have to tell him right off the bat that I saw colors around people and that I was psychic. I wanted to be sure whomever I talked to wouldn't send me away immediately.

I propped myself up on my bed with yellow pages in hand and flipped to the page with listings for the Dallas Gay and Lesbian Community Center. They had an information line that listed local classes and professionals in the area. I jotted down the first name and number of the first psychotherapist they listed. His name was Adrian. I dialed the number.

"Hi, this is Adrian."

I was startled to get a human voice.

"Um . . . hi," I stuttered.

"Hi back at ya." Adrian sounded amused.

"Yeah I got your name and I just came out and I need someone to talk to but here is the thing I am psychic and a massage therapist and

I don't really need someone telling me I am crazy because of the whole psychic thing; I mean I just came out and I'm a little freaked-out and well I guess you like specialize in that—well I mean not that you like *make* people come out but you know you like help them right?"

"Okay," Adrian said. "Slow down for a second. First of all, I have studied meditation and New Age texts in the past, so no worries. Why don't you tell me your name, and we can set up a session to talk about what you're looking for."

Adrian was a gay holistic therapist with whom I really identified right from the start. We got to work. The combination of traditional therapy along with my New Age studies did wonders. For the first time, I felt really grounded and centered; I became calmer and more dignified and at ease as we explored my life-changing event. I talked about everything. Not just the fact that I was gay, but my struggles with sexual abuse, my anger toward my parents, and my total lack of respect for myself physically. I'd had my "aha moment"; now I needed to learn to live a more harmonious life, one that incorporated all areas of life, not just the spiritual.

The first month after my announcement, I lost 30 pounds. Weight was just falling off me, and I didn't even change anything I ate. Every part of being suddenly became "more." Coming out was primarily about my sexuality, but it opened up so much more in me. I became who I truly was at the age of 19, which was a friendly, outgoing, funny guy. My announcement

> I'd had my "aha moment"; now I needed to learn to live a more harmonious life, one that incorporated all areas of life, not just the spiritual.

was so much more than "I'm a gay man." I finally started to identify with my physical person, my passion, my drive. Even my readings became stronger and clearer and more right-on. I started to get a small following. My ability to ascertain where someone was in her life was easier to verbalize.

I had been studying colors and auras for so long, and it was finally all coming together. For example, if I read for a woman with yellow or gold in her aura, I quickly realized that she would say many of the same things other women with gold or yellow in their auras had told me about themselves: She had difficulty in her relationships with men and a lot of power struggles. Men didn't know what to do with her; she was assertive and ambitious and often self-employed. People with yellow or gold in their auras don't hold back. They tell you what they think—but that doesn't mean they want the full and absolute truth in return.

> **People with yellow or gold in their auras don't hold back. They tell you what they think— but that doesn't mean they want the full and absolute truth in return.**

My latest readings confirmed the impressions I'd been getting for years. Every time I saw green, I listened to what people told me. "I am very creative," many of them said. So I made a note to myself: A green aura often means creative ability. Blue often means cheating and deception. When I see blue around a woman, I know that she's been cheated on. Not necessarily even with a lover. It could be a business partner; it could be a nanny.

And so on down the line. When I saw a certain color, I was perfectly confident in my predictions. And the people who came to me were amazed at my accuracy. My business started to shift: A typical work schedule had been giving five massages and two readings a week. As word of mouth grew, the balance started tipping, and I was thrilled. For a while, my clients were evenly divided; then, eventually, I was doing five readings and two massages every week.

My skin cleared up. I continued to lose weight. For the first time in my life, I really wanted to be in my body. I had spent so many years hating everything about my gawky, chubby 6'6" body, trying for as long as I could remember to just blend in. Massage school had helped me learn to accept and love my body, but overnight I started to really care about the image I presented. I joined a gym and started working out— and immediately went over the top with it.

I called my sister one afternoon to have her join me on a bit of a shopping spree.

"Tar, I want to go buy a treadmill."

"I'd love to look at them with you. I've thought of buying one as well."

Later that afternoon, we walked into an extremely large sports equipment store. Not exactly my favorite kind of shopping. The smell of rubber from sneakers and basketballs permeated the air. We walked up to a row of a dozen treadmills. Out of the corner of my eye, I could see an employee.

"Excuse me, sir. Do you work here?"

"I do," he replied.

"Great. I will take this treadmill." I pointed to the one I wanted.

"What!?" Tarrin screamed. "Are you crazy? Aren't you even going to test it out? Or go to another store? Or read some information on treadmills first? Or ask Dad? I thought you were just looking!"

"Well, I want one and I need one. I'll take it."

I've never been very good with money. (To this day, it's a struggle for me to budget.) My sister is the exact opposite. The princess of frugality was appalled at this latest example of the kind of behavior that tended to get me into trouble. We had spent 15 minutes, tops, in that store, and besides an expensive new treadmill, I walked out with sneakers and lots of proper workout clothes that looked cute—of course.

I attended therapy every week without fail and set myself mini-goals. One of the first tests was going to a gay bookstore and buying a coming-out book. That one took a lot out of me. I approached the counter and was barely able to stammer out, "I'd like a coming-out book." The bookstore manager was very kind. He'd heard it before. "Right over here. Oh, girl, I remember when I first came out to my mom. . . ." He was ready to chat all afternoon, but all I wanted to do was get out of there.

I cleaned out my closet—literally. I started doing the dishes and keeping my apartment clean and tidy. I bought a really powerful book called *Coming Out: An Act of Love,* and by chapter 4, I was so moved that I was compelled to come out to everybody, immediately. The safest way for me to do that was in writing, so I sent letters to everyone in my family.

I called my dad before I sent the letter. It was just a regular conversation; I wasn't planning on making any big announcement. While I was talking to him, I had a "psychic moment," which many people might interpret as a panic attack. My heart rate doubles. I can't even hear what the other person is saying, and my body becomes completely tingly. There are only two options when that feeling overcomes me: I can let the fear overcome me, or I can express what's going on in my body, and that will end it. So I said, "Dad, I have something to tell you."

My father heard the shift in my tone and became very quiet

on the other end of the line. He said, "Okay."

I said, "Dad, I'm gay."

What a surprise: He said, "I know." He continued, "Dougall, someone as handsome as you doesn't spend their life never dating. I knew something was up. So . . ." He hesitated for a moment. "Are you like RuPaul?"

"No, I'm White," I shot back. I had started getting quite a few questions like this. My sister wanted to know if I ever wore women's clothing. Sometimes I got highly offended, but they were naturally just curious. Tarrin told me, "You just spent so long saying, 'Don't go in my bedroom, and don't go into my closets.' I didn't know what was going on!"

> When I have a "psychic moment," my heart rate doubles. I can't even hear what the other person is saying, and my body becomes completely tingly.

Everyone in my family went through a short period of self-examination. My sister told me that she had left my house the night of my announcement, gone home, and thought to herself, *I'm a lesbian and don't know it.* When she went to bed that night, she looked over at her boyfriend and thought, *Bill's gay and doesn't know it. How could I have missed it—he's totally gay!*

My mother, too. She immediately thought, *I'm a dyke. I love jeans. I must be a total lesbian.* My dad, I think, didn't go through that process, but in a way everyone in my family had a brief, intense period of self-reflection and examination—a mini coming out. My extended family received my letters, and they all responded really well; I felt very blessed. Were they thrilled? No, but then again, it was hardly a big surprise.

I felt so much better, but meeting people once I came out was still tough. I was a young gay man who wasn't attending school, was self-employed, and had no gay friends. Many young adults come out in college, where there are youth groups or clubs and lots of opportunity to meet like-minded friends. I met people on the Internet. Cyberspace was a safe place for me to assume a personality and to experiment and figure out what was going on in this new world.

My next goal was going to a gay coffeehouse, sitting down and ordering a cup of coffee, and staying there long enough to drink it. I was so insecure; it was a whole new environment, and I hadn't spent much time hanging out with my peers in high school. I really had no idea what to do, but I had bonded with a friend on the Internet. He was older than I was, and I would never have guessed that he was just coming out. Kerry was my gay icon—out, dating, so cool. Really he was just more of an adult, more comfortable navigating this new world.

I listened, entranced, as Kerry told me stories about the people he had met in the Dallas gay bar scene. Because of my age, the topic of my joining him really never came up. Truth be told, I did not really enjoy alcohol at that time, not because it was illegal for me to order a drink but because—don't forget—I was a spiritual mentor. And any decent ethical guru would never allow a mind-altering substance to pass his or her lips.

But one day Kerry decided it was time for me to explore the options that the Dallas nightlife offered. Cedar Springs, an area of downtown Dallas, is the gay mecca of Texas. As we drove down Preston Road and made a left onto Cedar Springs, I felt the entire energy of Dallas changing. There were rainbow flags, charming boutiques, restaurants, bookstores, and, of course, plenty of what we'd come for: gay bars.

There are two main gay bars in Dallas. JR's was the hangout for gay men, and Sue Ellen's catered to lesbians. (It took me years to figure out that was a reference to the television show *Dallas*.) On this particular Friday night, I, Dougall Fraser, 19-year-old psychic to the stars—well, not really, not yet, anyway—was going to venture into the lion's den. I was consumed with worry about what I should wear. *Queer as Folk* was not yet on TV; there was no Will Truman on *Will and Grace* to emulate. I had never been to a gay bar. Forget gay bars— I had hardly ever set foot in any bar. Like a good WASP, I finally settled on a blue shirt and khaki pants—the Blockbuster Video employee uniform, basically. Remember, I was sheltered. Because of my height, I had no problem getting into JR's.

My heart was pounding. The bar was packed! Standing room only. I felt like I was surrounded by the most attractive group of men I had ever seen in my life. I did *not* feel worthy. Kerry noticed a group of friends across the room, and they motioned for us to join them.

"Hi, guys, this a friend of mine—Dougall," Kerry said.

"Did you say his name was *Giggle*?"

I was mortified. The bar was quite noisy, and my heart pounding in my ears wasn't helping. For a moment, I wasn't sure I could muster up the strength to tell this man that my name was not Giggle but Dougall. I was terrified to have come out and be standing in a gay bar. But I took a deep breath and reminded myself that I was in a place full of people just like me. People who for years had lived their lives in fear of being found out.

"It's *Dougall*, and I think I need a drink."

That night I had my first martini. Strong? Yes. Did the trick? Abso-fuckin'-

> I took a deep breath and reminded myself that I was in a place full of people just like me. People who for years had lived their lives in fear of being found out.

lutely! When that martini was gone, JR's did not seem nearly as scary; in fact, it seemed friendly, and I rather liked it. But we were just warming up; Kerry wanted to take me on a tour of all the gay bars on Cedar Springs.

I think there should be a reality show called *Gay Bar* because it is a truly fascinating world behind those doors. Across the street from JR's was the Roundup, a country-and-western bar. JR's had been a new experience, but this was a different planet. Standing on line waiting to enter, I realized my selected attire was not quite cowboy material. I had never seen belt buckles that big. Nor had I ever seen a gay man in tight, pressed jeans and a ten-gallon hat. Once we got in, Kerry and I stood at the huge bar and watched the action on the square dance floor in the center of the room. A line of men leaned against a wall around the dance floor, checking things out. Now, I have come a long way, and I am quite an advocate for gay rights, but still, the image in my head of two cowboys two-stepping . . . now, c'mon—that's just funny. At the time, it was mind-blowing.

After I'd watched couples two-step for about 30 minutes, my third martini was getting to me. Nature was calling. Kerry pointed me in the direction of the bathroom. I stumbled through and was immediately taken aback. It was an open room with a line of urinals, where two men stood next to each other peeing, their bodies only inches apart. Shocked does not begin to explain my reaction to this sight. I gathered my composure and moseyed up to an empty spot.

"Evening," one of the men said.

The man next to me is speaking as I pee? Is this normal? Do all gay men pee standing next to each other while having conversations? This cannot be. Does George Michael know about this? Both men glanced over at me momentarily, then returned to their business. There was not enough money in the world to get me to acknowledge the friendly salutation. I returned to Kerry to ask if this was standard in gay bar bathrooms. He told me it was not the norm. I told him I had had enough for the night, and he kindly drove me home.

Kerry and I had fun venturing out together, and I tried to figure things out. I didn't understand that in the eyes of the gay community, when someone first comes out, he's practically untouchable. They just look at you and know. "You just came out. You need to do your thing, go have fun." Someone who's newly out is not relationship material, but I didn't know that then. Now, of course, I totally understand it. When you first come out, you're like a kid in a candy store. You want to have fun; you want to experiment; you want to run around with every Tom, Dick, and Harry. It's just what you do. I went through my own adolescence in about 9 months—I was making up for lost time.

My body and my appearance continued to change for the better. I no longer went to Supercuts. I briefly went through an obsession with the gym and my treadmill and becoming the perfectly buff gay ideal. I transformed from grimy teenager to a guy who wouldn't leave the house unless I had on Gucci pants, slides, and highlighted hair and was freshly shaved and tanned. My sister started to sigh and ask me, "*Must* you check your hair every 37 seconds?" I had gone from one extreme to the other. I went from "I'm spiritual, I live in the mind, my physical body isn't important" to thinking shopping at the Gap stood for being hopelessly poor.

I was trying to figure out who I really was, though it was a confusing process. I was now giving readings to all kinds of people, talking about their marriages, how to get pregnant, sexual satisfaction. . . . Meanwhile, I was experimenting with sex, trying to figure out what worked for me. I didn't even know what kind of guy I wanted, but I had no problem advising everyone else on their love affairs.

I found it wasn't any easier for a psychic on the dating scene than anyone else. I was testing the waters, dating different types of people, and sometimes I'd feel the early warnings, but I ignored them the

> I found it wasn't any easier for a psychic on the dating scene than anyone else. I'd feel the early warnings, but I ignored them the same way everybody else does.

same way everybody else does. I could tell people why their boyfriend or girlfriend would never work for them, but when it came to myself, I was as blind as everyone else.

I'd been seeing a guy, very casually, for about 2 weeks when I went out to dinner one night with friends from my meditation group. Someone casually asked me, "So, how's it going with the new guy?"

I said, "It's not going to last."

"How do you know that?"

I answered, "It's fun, I'm enjoying his company, but we're just very different people and I know it's nothing permanent or lasting."

One friend of mine didn't like my attitude. "You shouldn't say that. You never know." He didn't think I was trying hard enough.

Of course, it didn't last. He was a good-time guy, drank heavily, partied hard until 4 every morning. We were out one night, and he took another guy's phone number right in front of me. We certainly weren't monogamous; he was free to go on other dates. But right in front of me was a little too much.

"Look," I said, "let's not do this anymore. It's not working. But I like you. I enjoy your company. Let's be friends."

The truth was that I didn't really even want to be friends with him. He was attractive and fairly good company, but once we removed a few beers and a movie, we really didn't have much in common. He also wasn't the most sensitive guy in the world.

"Do you mind if I lie about your job to my friends?" he'd asked me one day.

"What do you mean?"

"I tell my friends that you own a spa."

I supposed that was only stretching the truth, but the fact was that I was a massage therapist and part-time psychic. The third date into it, I knew it wasn't going anywhere. Even the first night, the night I asked him out, did I know in my heart it wasn't going to make it? I really did. But there's still a learning curve, and everyone needs to go through it. Even the people who know how it's going to end. We all have relationship lessons to learn. I was trying to figure out what I wanted in a mate. I learned it wasn't him.

I gravitated toward men in their thirties, and told myself it was because I was advanced and mature. Not even 20 years old, I was dating mostly 35-year-olds. In reality, I was avoiding people my own age because I was intimidated. I was supposed to be superhuman, psychic, a gifted healer—watch me! The truth of the matter was that I was actually younger in many ways than people my own age. I was behind— but trying hard to catch up quickly.

Chapter Seven

——◆——

IT'S MIDNIGHT
AND YOU NEED A FRIEND

BY THE NEXT SUMMER, 1 YEAR AFTER MY BREAKTHROUGH AT MEDI-
TATION CLASS, I HAD DONE SOME CATCHING UP. I had spent the year
dating and experimenting and growing up. I was out and proud of it.
If I happened to be in the grocery store and the checkout clerk asked
me what kind of bag I wanted, I'd say, "Paper. I'm gay." Word had
trickled back to Garden City, Long Island, and I was major gossip
fodder. "I hear Dougall is a gay witch living in Arkansas!" To be the
only person in my high school who had come out openly, not to mention a psychic . . . My lifestyle caused quite a commotion back home,
even though I was 1,000 miles away.

My massage business had all but withered away. I was doing five
psychic readings at my office for every massage client I still bothered
to book. With my newfound confidence, I had been working psychic
fairs over the past few months. Psychic fairs were held every Sunday,
and I auditioned by giving the person in charge of the fair a reading.
Once I broke into the circuit, I could work every single one—that is,
every one except the fair at Above and Beyond, the New Age store
where I'd been relieved of my cashiering duties. Theirs was the pre-

miere psychic fair in the Dallas area. I wasn't good enough for that one yet; I had to start smaller.

I had passed the test and was now permitted to rent a table at the various small fairs held around Dallas and Fort Worth. Renting a table cost somewhere between $50 and $75, which was a lot of money to invest at the time. It was certainly different to be on the other side of the table. We psychics would show up an hour before the fair began, and the roar of our engines would begin. I would take my star-and-moon tablecloth out of my briefcase (yes, some psychics have briefcases — well, all right, I was the only one) and smooth it down perfectly. I arranged my matching blue candles and brand-new business cards on its surface, then set up my professionally designed sign displaying my name and logo. My presentation, of course, was flawless.

Reading at psychic fairs was much like being a short-order cook. It was fast and furious. People wanted their answers, and they wanted them *now*. Families would come in together and race from psychic to psychic, looking for the answer they wanted to hear. Some of the others were a tough act to follow. This being Dallas, all my fellow psychics had huge, poster-size glamour shots of themselves on stands next to their tables, the kind picturing them wearing tons of makeup and a big hat, shot through a lens coated with Vaseline. These pictures looked *nothing* like the actual middle-aged women behind the tables. People would point at the portrait and say, "I'd like to get a reading from her," and the lady at the table would say, "That's me!"

> **Reading at psychic fairs was much like being a short-order cook. It was fast and furious. People wanted their answers, and they wanted them *now*.**

And everything they said, of course, came out in a deep Southern accent.

I sat at the table, closed my eyes, and meditated deeply, asking that only those who needed my guidance would come to my table. Then I was ready. I realized that I had plenty of competition directly across from me, next to me, and all around me. As much as psychics are there to help, we also all need to make a living. Out of 20 psychics I had gotten to know at the fairs, only one was actually supporting herself by working as a psychic full-time—Lexi.

Lexi was the undisputed queen of the fairs. As she walked in the door, her hair was teased 6 inches tall and ready to withstand a windstorm. She was in her fifties and always wore a black suit and dramatic gold false eyelashes, and had a Pan-Cake–covered face full of compassion. Lexi was the leader of the pack—the only psychic who always did 24 readings in a row. She had quite a following. She also had an attitude. At heart she was a really nice woman, but her ego had an aura that immediately jumped out at me. Her preferred color scheme was black and gold. For readings she sat behind a table covered with a black tablecloth with gold angels scattered all over it. She was destined to be either a psychic or a Solid Gold Dancer.

For months I observed her from the sidelines, fascinated. The organizers of the fair always tried to arrange the psychics so that there were a couple of card readers, a few palm readers, several clairvoyants, some astrologers. . . . They wanted everyone who attended the fair to have a nice variety from which to choose. One day I finally wound up with Lexi situated right in front of me. We smiled politely at each other as we set up, though I caught the look that wondered, *Who on earth is that child?* Lexi had stacks of flyers talking about how she had worked in the psychic industry for years, Jesus was a former client, yadda, yadda, yadda.

And then there was me. New Kid on the Block. Minus fake

lashes, glamour shot, and stilettos, I guess we were pretty even. Lexi was mobbed from the minute the fair opened. As usual, lots of people passed by my table, but my appearance confused them. I heard a lot of "I prefer to go to a woman." People seemed to be more comfortable with the idea of a woman hearing their most intimate problems. I also heard a lot of "You look awfully young." So I spent the entire day watching Lexi read for person after person. She held their hands as they cried after hearing the messages she imparted. I was amazed. I had to get a reading from her.

"Lexi, I'd love to trade readings with you."

"Why sure, honey. Aren't you just as sweet as you can be!" she drawled, and I do mean drawled. This woman had a Southern accent that made Dolly Parton sound like she's from the Bronx.

I was told to close my eyes and think of three questions. The first question that came to my mind was, Why do you wear fake gold eyelashes? Before I could think of two more, she began the reading.

"Honey, is there someone that died around you whose name starts with an F, an R, a K, or a D?"

"Um, well . . . my grandfather's name started with a D."

"Well, hot damn! I love when I am right!"

An F, an R, a K, or a D? What was this, *Wheel of Fortune?* For the rest of the reading, Lexi spoke in circles. Some hits, some misses, but what amazed and impressed me was that she never admitted a miss. Every time she got something right, she would cry out, "Hot damn!"

She charged more than any other psychic there, and the people really loved her. I could understand that. She was the Southern grandmother of the group. She believed in herself and gave good advice. To me she was pure entertainment. I spent many months working across from her every weekend, hearing hoots of "Hot damn!" every 15 minutes or so.

Looking back, I think most of the psychics at the fair were sweet.

Not all of them were terribly psychic, but they were trying hard to make a living and be good, honest people. For me it was basic training. I was learning how to differentiate a psychic impression from a miss. The difference was I admitted my misses. I also got to see the combination of a spiritual practice with the business world. That was always a bit uncomfortable for me. Someone like Lexi could make around $300 cash in a day, which is a great living. But you had to sell yourself. And I was just a kid.

Most of the psychics at the fair were sweet, trying hard to make a living and be good, honest people.

I had 5 seconds to make my pitch. "I'm a tarot card reader and clairvoyant. I'm going to read your cards, study your aura, and focus on the next year for you." That was all the time I had—people either sat with you or they didn't. Most often they didn't, but sometimes they stopped.

"What kind of readings do you do?"

I would explain to people my system, and my words would fall on deaf ears as they looked at my deck of tarot cards. "How old is your deck?"

"It's brand-new!" I would say with great pride. I was born in the late 1970s—newer is better to my people.

"Oh, well, Sandy over there clearly has a lot more experience—her deck is really worn in. I'm going to have a reading with her."

I had never considered that the quality of my readings would be affected by the brand or the wear and tear of my tarot cards. After that particular fair, I went to my sister's house for dinner, and for research I decided to give my deck that antique look. I actually put a spare deck of cards into her swimming pool overnight. I thought that perhaps if they were warped enough, my clientele would increase. It didn't, of course; the cards just looked like they had been drowned and then baked in the hot Texas sun. I realized in my mind that my success would have nothing to do with the age of my deck. I did not have to be like all of those other psychics around me. I needed to find my own voice and my own career path.

I had never considered that the quality of my readings would be affected by the wear and tear of my tarot cards.

Working the fairs was an excellent education. It taught me how to give a good reading, quickly, and really cut to the heart of a problem. Now and then, someone would take a chance and say, "Let's see what this kid has to say," and sit down. And when they did, I was dead on. I would come up with names and dates and specific predictions.

After I'd been working the fairs for a while, one man approached my table who was not exactly the typical psychic-fair type. He appeared to be about 50 years of age. He sauntered over with a sheepish look on his face that clearly said, "My wife made me come here." He was wearing brown dress shoes with no socks, khaki pants, and a white short-sleeved oxford shirt. As he leaned over the table to shake my hand, I was comforted by the familiar, fatherly scent of aftershave and Speed Stick.

"Hi there. Are you interested in a reading?" I asked.

"Yeah, my wife suggested I give it a try." He rolled his eyes.

"Well, take a seat. I promise to be nice."

As he sat down, I closed my eyes. At a fair there was no time for chitchat. We had 14 minutes left, and I needed to get started.

"Say your name, please, three times."

"Drew, Drew, Drew."

"Drew, when I look at you, I see numbers all over your energy. I also see the Count in my head from *Sesame Street*. Please answer yes or no: Do you work with numbers?"

"I am an accountant."

"Yes or no, Drew. It takes the fun out of it when you tell me things. Let me do the work," I laughed.

"Okay." He smirked. "Yes."

"You work in a partnership that is unfair to you in some way, yes?"

"Um, yes, that's true," he choked, clearly startled.

"Is it a family business?"

"Yes."

"You need to leave. Your family walks all over you. The business itself is dying, and you seem to be getting offers for other places of employment. You will start a job in 6 weeks that is much better."

"Wow, I'm starting a new job in about a month."

"Great, then you are a step ahead of me. What are some questions I can answer?"

"Can you talk about my wife, and do you see children?"

"Your wife is unable to have children at this time. She is way too consumed with it. Lovemaking is no longer about the two of you being together. For her it's a mission: Must conceive, must conceive. Here is your homework. For the next few months, use contraception when you make love. Focus on each other and being together. After the first of the year, stop using contraception but continue to focus on being with each other. When the stress of baby making is released, I think a child will be born."

"Wow—that's a good idea. Thank you."

As Drew stepped away from my table, I hardly had time to reflect on my thoughts before the next person sat in front of me. People had started to talk, and from word of mouth alone, I soon became one of the most popular psychics at the fairs. I would soon read for 24 people, back-to-back, all day.

Even the other psychics started to get readings from me, and, if I do say so myself, they were incredible. One day Lexi herself finally took me up on my offer. As she sat down, I looked right into her eyes and said:

"Lexi, there is a man around you. His name starts with a J. This is your soul mate."

"Well, hot damn! I just started dating a man named Jack!"

She got up from the table 10 minutes later, amazed, saying, "That was pretty darn good, Dougall."

I READ AT A PSYCHIC FAIR AT A WOMEN'S university while religious protestors waved signs out front. I read at bookstores and coffeehouses. Everything that a struggling 20-year-old psychic could do, I did it. This was around the time—late 1990s—that psychic phone lines were tremendously popular.

You couldn't turn on the TV without seeing an ad. They had always intrigued me; I thought it seemed like the ideal job for a psychic. I believed every word of the infomercials. It was my dream to work on a psychic hotline. It seemed too good to be true—I could work from home and do what I loved. I was hearing at the psychic fairs that some people were making $2,000 or $3,000 a month working psychic lines, plus bonuses. That was big money to me.

I called the Kenny Kingston Psychic Hotline and got hired on the spot over the phone. I didn't realize before, but it seemd like if you could talk, you were hired. They couldn't have cared less if you were psychic. I was in. I was asked to get a second phone line installed in my house and was sent a packet of information in the mail.

The way it worked was that I dialed in to an 800 number and heard a broadcast message. A woman would come on and say something like, "Hey, everybody, commercials are on at 11 tonight. We're going to have very strong hits between midnight and 3 A.M." All the psychics were arranged on a priority list, so when I started, out of 1,500 psychics who worked there, I was number 1,499. When someone wanted to call in for a reading, they were plugged in to psychic number 1. The second caller went to psychic number 2, and so on down the line. There would have to be 1,499 simultaneous calls for me to get one.

But I didn't realize that on my first night. The first time I logged in to the system, alerting them that I was plugged in and ready to receive calls, I was so excited! Of course, I was trying to be very spiritual. I had soft music on and candles lighted, and I was sitting with my tarot cards in front of me, ready for fire. Twenty minutes later, I kind of leaned back and relaxed a bit. An hour into it, I picked up a book. By 2 A.M. I had the radio on and was dancing around the room, wearing my headset. Finally, the phone rang at 4 A.M. I leaped on it. Protocol was to ask callers for their name and date of birth.

It was my dream to work on a psychic hotline. It seemed too good to be true—I could work from home and do what I loved.

"Kenny Kingston Psychic Hotline. My name is Dougall. May I please have your name and date of birth?" I said breathlessly, all in a rush.

The young man on the other end happened to be 18 on that very day (you had to be 18 years old to call a 900 number). It was ridiculous; I'm sure he was probably 13. He said, "All I want to know is when I'm going to lose my virginity."

I said, "You've got to be kidding me."

And he hung up. That was it. My first call. My only call, as it turned out, for the entire week. I was logged in to the system for 20 hours—from 11 P.M. until 3 A.M. five nights in a row—and received that one phone call. When I had signed up to work on the Kenny Kingston Psychic Hotline, I'd been promised that I would make between $12 and $24 an hour because I'd be paid by the talking minute. But if the phone didn't ring, I got nothing.

I called the office the day I got my check in the mail for my first week of work. My net pay was about $1.50. I complained, "I was online for 20 hours and only got one phone call."

The supervisor was very nice. She explained the whole priority process to me and said, "Well, I'll increase your priority and we'll see what happens." She bumped me up in the system to probably number 25 or so. That night I logged in, and the phone didn't stop ringing. As soon as I put the receiver down, a new call started ringing in. I did 10 readings an hour, from midnight until 4 in the morning. I literally could not get off the phone. I couldn't pee; I couldn't stand up—that phone rang every 7 seconds.

And the callers! They were on welfare; they were getting beaten by their husbands; they wanted to know when their sons were getting out of prison. I couldn't believe it. I hadn't thought that people who called psychic lines were necessarily the smartest or most sophisticated, but I met plenty of nice, normal people at the fairs and figured this would be more of the same. These callers were way out of my comfort zone.

First thing, 9 out of 10 callers would ask if they could speak to Kenny Kingston, the man they saw hosting the commercial. And those free minutes they were promised? I found out later that there weren't any free minutes. At least half my callers hung up after 2 minutes, when I would be right in the middle of saying something. This was because they thought they wouldn't be charged because they had seen the advertisement offering 2 free minutes. It was like getting kicked in the stomach each time someone hung up on me.

With the ones who stayed on the line, as I talked to them, I would say things like, "Ruth, I am sensing financial problems around you."

"What?"

"I am sensing financial problems around you?"

"Boy, say what?"

"Girl, money be bad?"

"Oh, yes, money be bad!"

I had to completely change my way of speaking. No more "I'm seeing intimacy issues and a romantic blockage." It was now "That man you hooking up with? He out." Nobody really wanted a reading anyway. They just wanted someone to listen to them, and apparently they didn't mind paying for the privilege.

When I logged out at 4 A.M. that first night after being bumped up, I was freaked-out. I could not even do it the next night—it was too weird and scary. The Kenny Kingston Psychic Hotline was not doing it for me. So I quit working for them and turned to a classier venue, the Psychic Friends Network. I had heard through some fellow seers that it was much better. I called the main office in Atlanta and spoke to someone in personnel.

The woman on the other end of the phone explained the whole Psychic Friends Network to me. I had to send in letters of recommendation, a picture, and a résumé. They required proof that whoever worked for them had been a practicing psychic for 10 years. This was a tough one for me; I was only 20 years old. So in my application I just left off my date of birth. I wrote a letter saying I had studied tarot, taught meditation and Reiki, and been a practicing psychic for 10 years. I got a call back from what I called ESP Central, and they set up three test readings. They were carefully screening me, and I was glad. My only worry was that I wouldn't meet their standards.

I dialed a number in Colorado for my first test reading.

"Hi, this is Alan. Is this Dougall?"

"Yes, sir. I'm a little nervous."

"Don't be."

"Alan, the first thing I see around you is blue. Did a relationship just end that involved the other party cheating?"

We were on the phone for about 10 minutes. He seemed genuinely impressed that I was able to target the demise of his marriage after he discovered his wife's affair. I was also able to come up with his current girlfriend's name and that he really didn't want to marry her. He was blown away. Then he went through his list of questions.

"What if someone called you and wanted to get their boyfriend back? Would you teach them how to put a spell on him?"

"Absolutely not," I said. "There is nothing anyone can do to help you get someone back if they don't want to be with you. You need to pray for the highest good for everyone concerned and make your peace with the situation." That was the right answer—he had to make sure I wouldn't manipulate the callers.

"What if someone asks for your home number and wants to talk to you privately for less money?"

That sounded just fine to me, but I knew that operators monitored the calls, so I said, "I would never do that! I'm here to make money for the Psychic Friends Network!" I was the perfect applicant.

I did another phone reading for another executive, who was pleased, and for my third reading, I read for the woman who ran the office of the psychics. I didn't get a good vibe from her; I couldn't connect with her. I could tell that she had a harsh personality and that men felt dominated by her. But I was 20 years old, applying for a job. What was I going to say? "You're intimidating, men don't like you, and you don't have a lot of friends. Hire me." So I ignored all that and did the best I could. And it was awful, a really bad reading. At the end of the session, she said, "Well, you're hired."

I was so surprised, I blurted out, "I can't believe you're hiring me. I thought that reading for you was really bad."

She was very blasé. "You did? No, don't worry. It was fine."

I decided to make up a name to use for my readings. I was already thinking ahead to a time when I might become a well-known psychic and might not want everyone to know I had done this. So I became Sean. And I have to say I felt much better about this new venture. The professional interview process had reassured me; I felt renewed optimism about being a phone-line psychic.

> I was 19 years old, applying for a job. What was I going to say? "You're intimidating, men don't like you, and you don't have a lot of friends. Hire me."

There is a constant, 24-hour-a-day stream of calls coming in to the Psychic Friends Network. But I learned that if I logged in during the middle of the day, when commercials weren't constantly running—let's say at 2 in the afternoon—I got only three or four calls an hour. I liked that pace. I hadn't liked working in the middle of the night, lonely souls pouring out their hearts at 4 A.M.; having breakfast at 2 P.M. This was more like regular working hours.

The people who called Psychic Friends Network were a more sophisticated bunch, though there were still a few who called and wanted to speak to Dionne Warwick. I'd be like, "Lady, I'm at home in my pajamas, and I've never met Dionne Warwick." No, I didn't really say that, but I wanted to. I used to turn on the TV across the room and monitor the commercials closely while I was logged in, to see at what point people started dialing in. Was it Dionne's tear that moved them? Was it when Vicki Lawrence was so wowed by her reading? The whole marketing process fascinated me. And even though I understood the business behind the whole entertainment aspect of the infomercial, a big part of me still wanted to believe in it.

The Psychic Friends Network certainly felt like the most reputable of all the psychic phone lines. With every paycheck, I received a whole sales sheet breaking out each of my calls, showing how long each person had stayed on the line, how many people had specifically requested me—everything. It was highly professional and organized on one hand, but I was starting to get pushed in a direction that made me uneasy. I was urged to sign my callers up for a special "club," so at the end of each call, I had to ask, "Would you like to join our Psychic Circle? For $9.95 a month, you'll get a voice mail system that gives you a free astrological reading every day!" I think what the company really wanted was a name and an address with a matching credit card number that could be automatically charged $9.95 every month.

I started getting bombarded with training brochures from the corporate office in the mail. It was never as flat-out as "How to Keep Callers on the Phone." They had cheery titles like "Ideas to Make Your Readings Better!" For example, start readings by asking your clients to count backward from 10 to 1 and center their thoughts. Well, that's an additional 10 seconds of time charged. I really wanted to believe that it was a good company and I was doing good work, but it was getting harder.

Let's say you as a caller decided to call the Psychic Friends Network. You would dial their 900 number and speak to a psychic who worked there. But say 2 hours later you're watching a commercial for the Nell Carter Psychic Hotline and decide to call there, too, maybe get a second opinion. You would dial a different 900 number and speak to someone else. But on my end, whichever number you dialed, my phone would ring. Whenever I lifted my handset, the first thing I'd hear was a whispered, "Nell, Nell." (Or "Psychic Friends," or "Kenny.") In the beginning, I didn't know what the little whisper meant, so I ignored it and said, "Psychic Friends Network. This is Sean. May I help you?"

The person on the other end of the phone was sometimes surprised. "Wait a minute. I just called the Nell Carter hotline."

"That's impossible. I work at the Psychic Friends Network." This happened a few times until I finally figured out what was going on. They were all the same company. If you called LoveLines, you got me. You called the Linda Georgian Psychic Hotline, you got me. You called Psychic Friends, you got me. All the smaller companies were merely divisions of the same big corporation.

From my impression, there seemed to be three huge corporations that owned three or more lines each. And the psychics who worked for one of these companies worked for them all. I quickly learned to catch that little whisper in my ear at the beginning of each call. It was to alert me to which number the caller dialed so I would answer the phone correctly. "Thank you for calling the Zodiac Hotline. . . ." "Thank you for calling Astrology Readings. . . ." All me.

I became further disillusioned but still wanted to believe I had a great job at a good company. But it was getting harder. I had a regular caller, Champagne, on the Psychic Friends Network. She called in every day at 11 o'clock and always requested me. She had the

> I really wanted to believe that it was a good company and I was doing good work, but it was getting harder.

same two questions for me every day: "When is my husband getting out of jail?" and "When am I getting my welfare check?" One day, I couldn't take it anymore. I said, "Champagne, the next time you want to call me, I want you to take $50, open a window, and throw it out. Because that's what you're doing every day. It is a complete waste of your money." She hung up on me in a huff, and that was the end of Champagne.

Every now and again, I'd get the frisky callers. I'd be saying, "As I'm turning over the cards, I see . . ." and they'd be interrupting every 5 seconds: "What are you wearing?"

Most of the callers really started to depress me. The last straw was when I started getting calls from people saying, "Sean, I got your letter saying you really needed to speak with me urgently . . ." and I'd say, "What are you talking about? I didn't send you any letter." They'd insist, "I have your letter right here. You're Sean at extension 5842, right?" I didn't worry about it too much until one day when I got a call from a woman who was livid.

"You sent my husband a letter, Sean. You said that you have important things to tell him about love and life and money." She paused, then really screamed, "My husband's dead! He just died of cancer! He was desperate. That's the only reason he would have called you! You don't have any fucking thing to tell him about love or life!" She really went off on me. I couldn't figure what all this letter stuff was about, so I called the line myself and posed as a caller. And 10 days later, I got a postcard in my mailbox, saying, "Dear Dougall, Your psychic Tom at extension 4821 needs to talk to you immediately about urgent matters concerning . . ."

I felt like a hooker. The ploy disgusted me. To this day, I believe that working one of those lines is one small step above being a prostitute. Those letters sent in my name were the end of it for me. Several years later, when I had achieved some success in the psychic world, I was offered my own psychic hotline. I turned it down flat. More than once, I have been offered a lot of money to lend my name to one. There is not enough money in the world for me to do something like that. Ever.

Those corporations were making millions and millions of dollars. They had more than 1,000 psychics working for them. The psychics were paid 15 cents for every minute they were on the phone, while callers were being charged $3.95 a minute. The biggest check I had ever gotten was for $195. My whole experiment with psychic hotlines lasted about 6 months, and over those 6 months, I tried working for them all. For a long time, I just couldn't let it go—the idea of doing my work, being psychic and helping people, from home, and the lure of good money. I kept thinking that I just had to find the right line and it would be the perfect job, but there was no good one.

> I felt like a hooker. To this day, I believe that working one of those lines is one small step above being a prostitute.

In my view, the Miss Cleo line was the worst. The worst. Apparently, as long as you had a heartbeat, they'd hire you. It later came out in a lawsuit against them that the United States government used to list them as an employer for people on welfare. Working a psychic hotline had become a guaranteed job. So while people in the media were investigating these hotlines and exposing their shams, the government simultaneously fielded complaints and used the hotlines as employment opportunities. The authorities knew that all of those people couldn't have been psychic. They should have been steering the people to phone sex lines or telemarketing, opportunities in which the consumer isn't paying for any particular talent.

And, man, these companies were raking in the bucks. In the middle of the night, my private line used to ring and ring, and when I finally picked up, there would be an automated voice saying, "Please log in now. The system is very busy." They were making tons of money.

Of course, the whole psychic hotline craze collapsed eventually in a maze of lawsuits. But I was done with it. I felt cheapened and abused and embarrassed. I was completely disheartened by the whole experience. Oh, there were talks around Dallas with friends of mine about starting our own line and doing things correctly, but I just couldn't see how it could be done. There's a reason it costs so much a minute—setting up the 900 number, getting advertising. . . . It takes a corporation. But if you had the capital to get started, you could make millions. Many did. Supposedly when the Psychic Friends Network started, they had only 50 psychics working for them, and they made comfortable money and had decent hours doing what they loved. But then everyone got greedy and it all went crazy.

I have experienced every aspect of being a psychic. Part of the reason I'm so confident in my abilities now is that I know what it's like to be treated like a fortune-teller. I know what it's like to be sitting hunched over your coffee table with a lit candle, waiting for your next call to come in. I know how it feels to sit behind a card table in a small New Age bookstore in a strip mall, hoping to get a $10 reading.

The whole psychic hotline experience was a big lesson for me: I know that even something as sacred as a psychic connection can be exploited for excessive profit, to feed someone else's enormous greed for cash.

More than anything, psychic lines taught me the power of television. So many people believe anything they see on TV. Anything! I understand that Dionne Warwick now has it written into her contracts that when she makes any kind of appearance, no one is allowed to ask about her psychic line. You are not allowed to even mention it. I can certainly understand why she might want to distance herself from it all.

Right around this time, I was praying hard. The psychic hotline thing was clearly over for good. My dad's financial assistance was going to end very shortly, and though I had a growing following, I wasn't making enough money to support myself as a psychic. I needed an answer. *I hate massage, I love doing readings. . . . How can I make a living doing what I love?*

I know that even something as sacred as a psychic connection can be exploited for excessive profit, to feed someone else's enormous greed for cash.

Three weeks later, I got a call from the *Dallas Observer*, saying they wanted to come take a picture of me to accompany an article they were writing about me. I had been named "The Best Psychic in Dallas." Now, why hadn't I seen *that* in my future?

Chapter Eight

BEST LITTLE PSYCHIC
IN DALLAS

PSYCHIC HOTLINE ADS HAD TAUGHT ME TO RESPECT THE POWER OF TELEVISION; I was about to learn about the power of the printed word. I have appeared on national television shows and all kinds of popular radio shows, and to this day I have never gotten anywhere near the response I did from a paragraph about me in a supplement of the *Dallas Observer*. It was a publicity explosion; it altered the entire course of my life.

"We're sending a photographer out to take your picture," the editor at the paper told me when he called to give me the good news. I had no idea how I had come to be chosen as the Best Psychic in Dallas, but I had bigger things to worry about. All I could think of was that my picture was going to be published in the paper for the world to see.

I was so excited. I thought I had hit the big time, but the experience of getting my picture taken was not the stuff of my dreams. By the time the photographer actually showed up at my office, I was beyond nervous. Most people don't like getting their picture taken to begin with. Well, that was nothing like knowing that thousands of people were going to see it. Look, it was the local rag in Dallas, Texas, but to me it was the cover of GQ. When he arrived, I asked anxiously, "Is a stylist coming?"

He was a brusque older guy who'd been around the block a few times. This was not any big assignment to him. He just looked at me. "You've got to be kidding." Then he got down to business. "I was thinking you could wear a turban and we could put 'Best Psychic' in an envelope over your forehead, like Carnac the Magnificent from the Johnny Carson show."

All right, so it wasn't the cover of GQ. But Carnac—I didn't even get the reference. I had my little Buddha statue at the ready and told him I really wanted it in the shot. He wasn't sure that would work. We started with some test shots, and I tried my damndest to look straight into the camera and present the image I imagined people wanted to see: a centered, unified being from whom divine love radiated. I'm sure it looked more like a mug shot. I was petrified.

It was so scary that in a minute or two, the photographer said, "I think we should try some with your eyes closed." It was that bad. He was not happy. "Come on, relax. . . . You look too stressed."

Of course I was stressed—he had lights all over, and he was pushing me around. We were an hour into what was supposed to be a simple photo shoot, and he had nothing he could use. Finally he posed me against a large mirror I had in my office. I was supposed to rest my hands and stare into it as if I were gazing into another world. He kept moving my hands around and barking, "Relax your hands!" He was very impatient, and I was on the verge of tears. So I closed my eyes and heard the camera go off. I just wanted this to be over. I hated him.

Looking back, I should have just gone with the turban.

In the weeks before the "Best of Dallas" issue hit the stands, I had numerous nightmares about what the article would say about me, how my photo would look, and what people would think of me afterward. Not the kind of nightmares that would take circles of psychotherapists to analyze, they were the most awful, yet simple, bad dreams expressing shame and fear that I'd ever experienced.

Each dream began the same way. I was reading a copy of the *Observer*, thumbing through it with increasing agitation as I looked for *my* article. Sometimes I was on the cover with a big red *fraud* written across my forehead, but I wouldn't realize that until I'd gone through the whole magazine and started over. In my favorite prepublication nightmare, I turned a page and found that the editors had pasted my face above the body of a buff, shirtless guy with bulging biceps. The caption read: "Sexy Psychic!" I was mortified. "That's not me," I cried out in the dream. "That's just not me!"

I woke up breathless and sweating. How could I be so scared? What was my problem? I don't know. But I was that frightened. No one had ever written about having a psychic experience with me. My psychic ability was the one source of public recognition and pride in my life. I thought my being a psychic was easier for people to accept than my being gay. I was pinning all my life's hopes on the psychic angle. But now a core part of my identity had been put under the microscope. I would be analyzed, dissected, and judged. Maybe the article would be critical of me. Or poke fun at me.

"I'm not ready!" I shouted, but again the universe was not listening. The story and accompanying photo came out about 6 weeks after my photo session. The editor at the paper had alerted me the day before it came out, so I raced over to my local

> My psychic ability was the one source of public recognition and pride in my life. But now a core part of my identity had been put under the microscope.

bookstore the moment it opened on the big day. I grabbed the paper
and flipped frantically through it, and was shocked when I saw how
much space my section took up. The piece was a multipage roundup
of "the best" of Dallas—best dry cleaners, best desserts, best hairstylist,
best coffeehouse—there were tons of listings. But my picture took up
a half a page with an accompanying article. I was freaked-out. Of
course, they spelled my name wrong—"Dougal" with only one L—
because everybody always does. But the article itself allayed all my
fears. It read:

> Topping out at 6 feet 6 inches and a baby-faced, weirdly ma-
> ture 20 years, Dougal Fraser is the Dallas psychic with the bur-
> geoning national reputation who during one 45-minute reading
> is likely to regurgitate five years' worth of therapy over the tarot
> deck. Fraser is also a licensed masseur who operates a holistic
> services office with his sister Tarrin. Fraser's witty, down-to-earth
> assessments of your aura and your future are likely to convert
> die-hard skeptics. If this guy isn't truly clairvoyant, he's intuitive
> as hell, and in the end, what's the difference?

I noted the writer's name and realized how all this had come to
pass. It had been just another day at the office for me a couple of
months earlier when a young gay man had booked a reading. He had
mentioned that he was a writer, but I didn't ask if he'd been published.
A lot of young writers haven't been. No point in starting out on a low
note. While we were talking about his life in general terms before the
session, I flirted with him a little. I couldn't remember what he had
asked me or what I predicted for him, but I did recall strongly that it
had been a great session. He had seemed pleased when he left, but he
never called back, so I didn't think any more about him.

That one reading had certainly paid off for me in a very big way. Gleefully, I repeated the phrase "best psychic in Dallas" over and over silently to myself. I bought a dozen copies and raced to my sister's house. We sat by the pool, lounging and reading it over and over again.

"This is fantastic!" my sister said, laughing in delight. "Mom is going to freak."

"Do you think I look thin? You don't think I look fat, do you?"

"Would you stop!"

From her house, we called to check our office voice mail. "Your mailbox is filled!" the electronic voice said. *Filled!* "I read about you in the *Dallas Observer*. . . ." True, the system held only 30 messages, but we'd never in the history of our office had 30 messages piled up before. I emptied the mailbox, scribbling down all the names in a spiral notebook, and an hour later, when I checked in again, the electronic voice said once more: "Your mailbox is filled!" *Filled!* "As soon as I saw your picture, I knew you could help me. . . ."

This was unbelievable. Tarrin and I looked at each other in amazement. Suddenly I said, "Tarrin, I just got a flash. I'm going to be on TV." I knew it as clearly as I'd ever known anything.

The messages went on and on. Between returning phone calls, I was rushing to Federal Express offices, sending out at least 20 copies of the *Dallas Observer*, at $30 a pop, to everyone in my family across the country. (I am still a man of instant gratification. If I'm on the phone ordering something from a catalog, the overnight delivery is sooo tempting. Almost every spiritual mentor has lectured me on the importance of patience. Yet I seem to overlook that lesson every time it's taught.) How could I not send those magazines overnight delivery? My life had literally changed overnight. I was excited, on an energy high.

I was the best little psychic in Dallas—and I was loving it.

The next day, I had the first full day of readings in my career, eight sessions booked back-to-back. It was exhausting. And it was followed by another full day and yet another, and so on into the foreseeable future. I sat in my office reading for people much older than I was, advising them on life experiences I personally had never experienced. In the background, the phone rang repeatedly. I was booking around eight appointments a day, 5 days a week.

When I checked the messages between sessions, the electronic voice announced, "Your mailbox is full!" I couldn't listen to all of the callers before my sister would announce, "Dougall, your 4 o'clock is here." *Will my husband come back to me?* "Your mailbox is full!" *Should I ask my boss for more money? Please tell me why I want to kill myself.* How do I know that I'm saying the right things to people in such distress? "Your mailbox is full!" *My father molested me, but I have been repressing the memory of the details.* I looked at one sweet-looking woman client and clearly saw two men in her life. "Why do I see two men?" I asked, afraid I was suffering psychic double vision. "I'm having an affair," she said. Within 2 weeks, I realized that half of Dallas was cheating on its mates. Suddenly all those country-and-western songs made sense.

At the end of every day, I was completely drained of energy. I had piles of Post-it notes representing unreturned phone calls. I was amazed at how much I had talked and how intimately I had shared with people about their lives—and how discouraged about the state of humanity I was afterward. Within a few weeks, I realized that trying to conduct eight readings a day, 5 days a week, was a bad idea. I knew that exhaustion following any kind of spiritual work was a sign I might be doing something wrong. As a clear channel, I should be feeling uplifted at day's end or, at the least, no more tired than anyone working an 8-hour day.

But I kept booking that heavy schedule for longer than I should have, for two reasons: (1) Working a full day is what you do in America, if you absorbed any of the Puritan work ethic while growing up—and I did; and (2) Money. Oh, yes, the tricky issue of money. I was making $75 a session.

Suddenly I shopped. My mantra became "Banana Republic." I spent the money almost as fast as it came through the door.

Whether money is a good or an evil is the issue I have wrestled with from day one as a psychic. How does one charge for something that is supposed to be a gift? If we lived in a society where I could barter and trade services for goods and other services, a society where rent, taxes, and the cost of living were not motivating factors for getting out of bed in the morning, my fee scale would be different. But we don't, so how much do I charge? What is fair? I want to live well. I want to respect clients. And I want to be affordable.

I must have been affordable because I was booked well over a month in advance by the time a new issue of the *Dallas Observer* hit the stands. One day as I was booking an appointment, the full impact of my new situation hit me. Only the previous month, I would have said to the woman calling for a session, "I can see you tomorrow at 2." And I would have spent at least 15 minutes on the phone with her as she negotiated a more favorable time that day or shared with me her anxiety about "seeing a psychic." Often I was put in the uncomfortable position of encouraging business like an evangelist at the tent flap. *Come on in! You'll like it!*

Now, in mid-October, I said to the caller, "The next available appointment is December 18 at 3 P.M." "I'll take it!" she said. "I'm so glad you can see me!" Hanging up the phone, I marveled at her reaction and the speed with which she had gone from a voice on the phone to a name on the calendar. Some of the people who called told me how delighted they were to speak with me personally, giggled nervously, and seemed genuinely pleased to hear I was doing well.

Others insisted that they *must* see me immediately.

"But I have an emergency!" was a frequent lament.

> I never knew there were so many psychic emergencies. What exactly constitutes a psychic emergency? You're stuck in another world? Your house is haunted? You're in labor with your own rebirth?

I never knew there were so many psychic emergencies. What exactly constitutes a psychic emergency? You're stuck in another world? Your house is haunted? You're in labor with your own rebirth? I can't begin to imagine what a true psychic emergency would be. I wasn't sure how to respond to them. Did I rearrange my schedule, making someone else wait for a later appointment, to accommodate this "emergency"? Did I fit them in after regular appointments? Now I realize the "best hairdresser" and "best chiropractor" in Dallas were confronting the same weighty issues, but then I thought I was special. And the weight of being special is heavy.

I searched my soul, trying to figure out how to handle these people with emergencies. *What*, I asked myself, *is in both their and my highest good?* After turning myself into a clairvoyant contortionist to suit their needs, I discovered that the client with a "psychic emergency" was not quite the person I wanted to see, or even should see. Typically that person needed a professional therapist—and fast. I kept a list of qualified therapists and gently sent that type of caller away.

In fact, I suggest to most clients that they spend a little time with a counselor or a therapist or a life coach. After our sessions, I feel like I've opened a Pandora's box for them, leaving them with impressions and predictions that they need to sort out and work through. I say, "Here's where you're going, and here's where your roadblocks lie." That's like walking into a teenager's messy room and pointing out what needs to be done without giving them any guidance on how to do it.

Besides, everyone should have a period of reflection or inner search in their life. It just probably shouldn't last as long as Woody Allen's therapy has.

On a Friday at the end of October, I got the call I knew was coming. Television. Yes, television was calling me. I returned a message from a man who identified himself as the producer of a local morning show. He said, "I read about you in the *Observer*." I began to tremble and hoped my voice wouldn't quaver. "Could you come in and talk to me about possibly appearing on our 'little' show?"

Little! Little? In my mind, "little" meant a cable-access show produced in somebody's basement or at a local mall on weekends. Anything on an actual network was a big deal. Eagerly I agreed to come in for what I know now was a "preinterview." Remember, they'd never seen a photo of me with my eyes open. They really needed to check me out. If I had nightmares about the article before it appeared, they paled beside the dreams to come. I was going to be on television! Never mind it was a local morning show; to me, at 20, it was practically *Good Morning America*.

My mood bouncing from exhilaration to stark fear, I met the producer in his office at the appointed time. Actually I was early, but I waited outside the building until the correct time to walk in.

He shook my hand and said hello, then immediately asked me

for a reading—right there in that open, crowded space with cubicles separated by half walls in lieu of real offices. I remember that reading as being absolutely awful. He didn't want me to use the tarot cards that I'd brought along as props to keep my hands busy. *How am I to do this?* I wondered. *What am I going to do with my hands?*

"I see a lot of gold in your aura," I said. He didn't ask me what that meant, which was not a good sign. If he'd asked, I could have told him it was a powerful, masculine color.

The reading lasted approximately 15 minutes. He showed no expression at all, made no comments, asked no questions. I'd never seen such a blank face. I could imagine him being quite good in an old-fashioned Texas poker game.

And because I'd never read in such a chaotic environment, I had no confidence in the impressions I was getting about him. People were walking past, conversing with one another, calling out questions across the room. Phones were ringing.

"That was a good reading," he told me when I'd finished. "It was quite accurate." I couldn't believe my luck and relaxed slightly. He opened his appointment book, picked a date 2 weeks ahead, and said, "I've got you down. That's it."

I was booked! And I was in a panic by the time I hit the street. The nightmares began again that night. Now I was on television with the big red *fraud* as my identifying logo. The following day, I called the producer and said, "I really think doing a taped segment is a better idea, don't you?" If I was truly awful on tape, they wouldn't air the segment and I would be spared the humiliation.

"No, I don't," Mr. TV said. "Live." Live! "Don't bring your tarot cards," he said. Live! And no props. "We'll be talking about the Dallas Cowboys."

In shock, I hung up the phone. Oh, this was worse than my worst nightmare. I'd devoted my leisure time to the avoidance of sporting events. Now, in my television debut, I would have to talk like "one of the boys." Didn't he suspect I might be gay? Was he oblivious? Or did he see the humor in a gay psychic predicting the fate of the Dallas Cowboys? They play football, right?

I went to sleep that night whining, "Can't we make predictions about something I know about, like fashion?" My dreams over the next 2 weeks were studies in terror. In one recurring dream, the interview was going well except for one problem: Foam kept coming out of my mouth and dripping all over my chest. During the commercial break, a makeup person mopped my chest with a sponge. And the announcer said, "Next up, our foaming psychic."

> **Did the producer see the humor in a gay psychic predicting the fate of the Dallas Cowboys? They play football, right?**

🖎 **ON THE DAY OF THE SHOW, THEY HAD ME COME IN EARLY TO READ FOR THE ON-AIR FIELD REPORTER OFF CAMERA.** When I got there, I learned that the reporter would also be interviewing me on camera because the news anchors had refused the assignment. Such a thing was too undignified for them.

He was a trophy reporter, handsome in a plastic way. As soon as he walked into the room, my psychic impression was that he had a problem with money, was unfaithful in his relationship, and was generally shallow and fake.

That was the first time I said to myself, *I hate reading for the talent*, but it was certainly not going to be the last. You can't tell the talent anything like the whole truth because you need to make them look good to the audience and hope they return the favor. I began by checking his aura, the way I begin all readings.

"You have a lot of mint green in your aura," I said.

"Mint green?" he sniffed. He knew I was gay.

"Yes," I said, oozing sincerity. "In a man, mint green is a color of youthful outlook and energy and great sexual appeal to women." It's also a sign of immaturity, hyperactivity, and a guy with a Casanova complex.

"Really," he said. His chest puffed out. "What do you see in my future?" By the time I told him I saw him having opportunities in other areas of entertainment around the end of the year, he loved me. (He did have a bit part in a movie and a short-lived stint as a local car dealership spokesman. Hey, I didn't tell him he was going to be wildly successful in those opportunities!)

Sitting across from him on air, I was glad we'd done the reading. It made him predisposed to be kind to me. Still, I didn't think the segment went well. Any time you put a gay man with body issues in front of a camera, he will tell you, "That didn't go well." How could it go well when I didn't look as thin and handsome as I'd hoped I would? (I checked the monitor.) We talked about the Cowboys. The one question I remember is "What do you see happening for Barry Switzer this year?" Barry Switzer was the coach of the Dallas Cowboys, but I didn't know that. I predicted that he would move on in a different direction. "I don't see him a part of the team much longer," I said. The trophy weatherman laughed.

But I was right. Switzer was fired that year. And not incidentally, I received well over 100 calls from people who wanted to book readings after that 3-minute segment.

More television bookings, including repeat appearances on the same show, followed. There were radio interviews and newspaper stories. My appointment book was filled so far ahead that Banana Republic seemed to be in no danger of reporting a bad fiscal year.

But everything depended on my keeping the magic alive in the sessions with clients. Somehow I was able to make all the public hoopla go away when I shut the office door. At the end of the day, however, I was still neurotic Dougall.

Chapter Nine

THE EMPEROR
HAS NO CLOTHES

THE *DALLAS OBSERVER* ARTICLE HAD BEEN MY SIGNAL FROM THE
UNIVERSE that being a psychic truly was the right career choice for
me. For years, I had never believed that my childhood hobby could
actually morph into a job and a well-paying career. It had never
seemed possible to be psychic and yet live a well-balanced, successful
life. I was now doing that—succeeding—but what I was struggling
with was balance.

My massage business disappeared in the flurry of print articles,
television shows, and radio appearances. People who had been
coming to me for years for a standing appointment on Mondays at 6
were now told that they'd have to wait 2 months for a massage appointment. I charged twice as much for a 45-minute reading as I
would have for a massage, and I was booked solid 3 months in advance. Massage as a career was finally over, and I couldn't have been
happier about it.

I hired an assistant to book my appointments, closed down the office, and went looking for a new apartment. I settled on a loft in a
trendy downtown Dallas location. The building had originally been

---

For years, it had never seemed possible to be psychic and yet live a well-balanced, successful life.

---

a department store in the 1920s and now housed successful young urban professionals—which I suddenly was. The building had security, a doorman—you name it. I had arrived. I set up a Japanese fishbowl dining room table, where I did readings, and designated a certain section of the loft, the area just beyond the entrance, as my work space. I now saw clients at home.

After the initial period of exhausting myself with eight appointments a day and completely burning myself out, I set a pricing plan and figured the optimal number of readings per day that would allow me to be as present for my clients as possible. Doing eight sessions a day had been impossible—by the time I got to the last session, I was hardly in the room. I was dancing somewhere in the cosmos, just waiting to go home.

Eventually I settled on five sessions a day. That seemed fair, to my clients and to me. It gave me time to run the business end and also to sleep late. Ah, the perks of self-employment.

I was spending my days in meditation and counseling clients. I was doing good work that I was proud of and making good money, too—but my nights were a different story. For years, I had tried to reach the highest possible level of enlightenment, constantly exhorting myself to be "spiritual." Through therapy and coming out, I realized that the earth is a wonderful place and there are other pleasures besides the spiritual. I'm all for showing up at a Native American drumming circle, but it was equally fun to go out with my friends and dance until 4 A.M. Did that make me a fraud? I struggled to reconcile the two halves of my being—spiritual guru and successful young single guy.

"SHELLY, AS WE CLOSE YOUR SESSION, I WANT YOU TO REMEMBER THAT GOD WOULD BE SO MUCH KINDER TO YOU than you are to yourself. You are hurting yourself by staying in this relationship. Honor yourself this week; take care of your body." It was a Friday night, and I was finishing up my last appointment of the day with a client I liked who had some serious problems with self-esteem, an abusive relationship, and body issues.

"You are so right, Dougall. I love hearing your thoughts. You make me feel so much better."

For a minute after Shelly left, I could feel her soul present in my loft. I closed my eyes and drifted away for a moment, then was startled out of my reverie by the phone. I scrambled to get it.

"Hello?"

"It's Kerry. I had an awful day at work. JR's has dollar margaritas tonight—want to meet there in 15 minutes?"

"I'm there."

As I walked through the door of JR's, my perception was totally different from that of the kid who had been afraid to even enter. I was now of legal drinking age. I was more comfortable in my skin—in fact, to tell you the truth, I walked with a bit of a strut. Kerry hadn't shown up yet, a circumstance that a year ago would have sent me into a downward spiral of shame and insecurity about being in a bar alone. But now I felt totally comfortable. The air in that bar exuded sexuality. Darting eyes, casual smirks—Shelly's issues were the furthest thing from my mind. *Margarita* was my mantra. I ordered a drink and pondered for a moment.

A small voice in my head nagged me: *Dougall, you should be at home, resting and meditating. You have five sessions tomorrow, and you're supposed to do a lecture at a holistic fair in the morning.*

But it's Friday night! I thought, inwardly pouting. I wrestled with this voice all the time. Was I a true spiritual mentor? It didn't feel that way now as I stood at the bar, hoping to God the cute guy across the way would offer to pay for my drink.

> **Was I a true spiritual mentor? It didn't feel that way now, as I stood at the bar, hoping to God the cute guy across the way would offer to pay for my drink.**

"You look spaced-out," Kerry said from behind me.

I turned and smiled. "It's been a long day."

"What's the matter—tired of vacuuming your magic carpet?"

Of course, underneath the jokes, my friends were supportive of my career, but they never missed a chance to make fun of it. (I now have a rule when I meet new people. You get five jokes. And use them wisely, my friend. None of this "Did you know I was going to say that?" Believe me, I've heard them all.)

Kerry and I grabbed our drinks and headed off to see if other friends were around. As I walked up the stairs to the outside patio, I heard my name.

"Dougall, is that you?" Shocked does not begin to describe the tone of the woman's voice. Her eyes were wide, and she nervously pulled on the strap of her Prada bag.

"Yes—oh, hey, Shelly. . . ."

"What are you doing here?" she asked.

"I'm meeting some friends." Now the sarcastic part of my mind wanted like to retort back to her, "Why are *you* in a gay bar . . . alone?" But I refrained. At this very moment, I had to straddle my two worlds carefully; they had just come face-to-face. Shelly looked up to me as her mentor, someone who had all the answers.

"I just can't believe you're here."

"Well, Shelly, I am human. I need to relax and have fun."

"But what about all that stuff you said about taking care of my body?"

"I meant that. I still do."

"I have to say I'm really disappointed in you." And she walked off.

If I had accidentally run into Shelly 6 months before, I would have been overcome with shame—dropped my drink, told her I must have lost my way, and asked her for directions to the nearest Buddhist monastery. But I was tired of the pressure of my own standards. For the first time, I had admitted that I, too, had had a stressful day and wanted to get out of my own head, at least for a moment or two. I felt such a strange sensation in my body: part fear, part exhilaration. Was I a disappointment? Was it wrong for a young, red-blooded gay man to meet his friends for cocktails after work? Did a reaction like this mean I had to be different? Could I live in both worlds?

I honestly wasn't sure. But by the third margarita, I decided that at least for the moment, this world was better. We were laughing and dancing without a care in the world. All right, I said I would be honest—it was my fourth margarita.

That night was filled with everything it should be for a 21-year-old single guy. I got numbers from men I would probably never see in the light of day. Kerry and I gossiped the night away and had a terrific time. But Cinderella had chores in the morning.

When the alarm clock rang in the morning for the 10th time, I realized I had used up all the possible snooze time. I had a small speaking engagement at noon. I rolled out of bed, and as my feet hit the cold concrete floor, there was a sudden sharp pain in my head, quickly reminding me that dollar margaritas are really not such a bang-up idea.

The condemning voice in my head started up right on cue: *What kind of spiritual mentor wakes up with a hangover? Maybe it's not a hangover? Nah, I probably have a cold. Or a tumor, or small gremlin-like creatures living in my skull, hacking away at the core of my being.*

But my haggard reflection in the mirror confirmed the diagnosis: hangover. My soul was consumed with guilt. I hopped in the shower, hoping to wash away my sins.

After my shower, I had 2 hours to pull myself together before I was scheduled to speak at a fairly large holistic fair in the Metroplex. I did not feel worthy, even though for all intents and purposes, I was the new Lexi. I had a following. I had a long waiting list of clients. I was now well-known on the small-psychic-fair circuit. There were many people who were genuinely interested in what I had to say, but at the moment I was feeling far from genuine. I sat on the edge of my bed and looked closely at the beautiful home I had acquired. I deserved this, didn't I? And I deserved to live the kind of life any normal 21-year-old guy wanted, didn't I? The look of betrayal on Shelly's face flashed in my mind, and I felt a pang of guilt.

Dougall, focus! I closed my eyes and breathed in deeply. My consciousness became bigger than my loft. I no longer heard the sounds of the busy city surroundings. I became one with my soul.

Dear God, I asked, *what am I to do? I am so torn. Do you want me to live my life as a monk? The idea of only seeing the future and always being holy is just too hard. I can't do it anymore; I need more.* My head was still pounding, and I was overwhelmed with guilt. I sat on my king-size bed with its Ralph Lauren sheets and prayed with all my heart.

A feeling of peace suddenly flooded my being. I felt a sense of satisfaction and warmth as I envisioned the group I would be addressing that Saturday afternoon. *I can be both things* were the words that flowed through my mind. They were almost dancing around my hangover. In that moment I decided that from this point forward, I would be as honest and authentic as possible. I would no longer try to perpetuate a "gurulike" image—I would be real and authentic. I did not need to be perfect in order to be holy; in fact, what makes me holy are my flaws.

In the car ride over to the convention center, I realized that this epiphany did not give me license to drink myself blind every night without a care in the world. I must maintain responsibility, but I would now give myself permission to be fully human. I repeated it over and over again in my mind: I allow myself to be human, with all the mistakes and desires and good times and embarrassment that come with it. I had always thought that to be spiritual or to be holy meant sacrifice. Sacrifice of sex, and silliness, and material goods, and every other fun thing in the world. I had taken the look in Shelly's eyes as a rebuke,

I did not need to be perfect in order to be holy; in fact, what makes me holy are my flaws.

that I should be *holy*, when in fact, I realized now, I should take it as an even bigger message: I should accept every part of my being. This was a tremendous breakthrough in my thinking; I had not felt such a clear message since Camp Dudley.

I parked my car and entered the fair. As the woman in charge announced the next speaker—me—I looked at the group of 30 or 40 people who were sitting in chairs, waiting patiently to hear me speak about auras. I glanced at the program to remind myself of the topic. As usual, I had nothing typed up or prepared. I never bring notes for speeches; I prefer to let the energy of the moment move me.

Instead of standing at the podium, I grabbed a chair and sat in front of the group, at the same level as my audience. There may have been a little "I'm okay, you're okay" feel to this—no gurus here! But in truth, I get insecure about my height. The last thing I need is to be on a stage, towering over everyone like some cypress tree. Today of all days, I wanted to be one with my audience, not up on a pedestal. I began:

"Hi, everyone. I am not special."

I spoke for about 30 minutes about my beliefs. How I had struggled with what it means to be psychic and what it means to be spiritual. Each word made me feel more invigorated. Each word made me feel more connected to every person I made eye contact with. And they responded to my honesty. Not with words, but I could see it in their nods. They understood; they related to me and my story. I admitted my doubts; I admitted my fears of being wrong. I finished by telling them that I trusted in God. God: a word that I did not use very much. But it's true. As much as I am a teacher on this planet, I am also a student, and for the very first time, I spoke out about it. I felt humble yet powerful.

After my brief talk, it was time for audience readings. There was a new calm in my body. I closed my eyes to connect, so to speak. For a moment, I could feel the part of me that was a hungover young man, so I called upon the divine me. We all have a higher self, which is the way that God created us, wise beyond our years. As I focused on my highest good, I could feel the pull of the people in front of me. I knew I would begin with a man. I opened my eyes, and directly in front of me was a young man around the same age as me.

"I would like to begin with you. Please stand and say your name."

"I'm Josh."

As Josh stood, he elongated like a gazelle. He was much taller than I had expected. Such a simple movement was filled with subtle grace. He had long, lean muscles like a dancer; his demeanor was shy and humble. His aura was a brilliant icy green.

We all have a higher self, which is the way that God created us, wise beyond our years.

"Josh, the first color I see around you is an electric green. This is the color of the creative nature. It is also the color of youth and vitality. Do you work with children?"

"Sort of."

"Are you a dancer?"

"Yes."

I am not sure if I knew he was a dancer because I am psychic or the way he presented his body. In that moment, what's the difference? When I embrace someone's energy, I take every part of them in.

"Why do I see children connected to your career?"

"I am part of a ballet company that works and performs in schools."

"Okay, I see now."

Many times, seeing something psychically is like reading a book jacket. I get the overall theme of someone's life but have to read on, ask questions, to help me pull it together.

> Many times, seeing something psychically is like reading a book jacket. I get the overall theme of someone's life but have to read on, ask questions, to help me pull it together.

I informed Josh that he was in the right place in his life. He had reached his target by combining his dance skills and his ability to connect with kids. As I shared this knowledge, he sat down with a smile. I did a couple more sample readings that felt very genuine, accurate, and complete. When I walked off the stage, the sensation of my hangover returned, but for a moment, the divine consciousness had come through me because I had faith that it still could. I wanted more of this.

BY THIS POINT, I HAD BECOME A REGULAR AT THE FAIRS IN DALLAS. I was, if I do say so myself, very popular, the main attraction, the one who did 24 readings back-to-back. My slots were filled quite quickly. And then one day I got the call. Above and Beyond had invited me to their fair! I had arrived.

My first day at Above and Beyond, there was a sense of pride when I learned I would be in the large classroom. That's right, folks—the same pimply-faced kid who had been fired from this store, the one who insisted that all classroom distinctions were absolute BS, was now holding court in the large classroom!

Obviously the title of "Best Psychic" helped me quite a bit. When customers entered Above and Beyond for the fair, they were given a brochure of all of the psychics available that day. When people saw "Recognized as the Best Psychic in Dallas by the *Dallas Observer*" next to my name, they instantly wanted a reading from me. Membership has its privileges. It was a bit awkward for the other psychics, too, the ones I had studied and admired in this very same store. A few of them were jealous; I heard that some of them were accusing me of making up that title. I photocopied the article itself for proof. Now I really was Lexi, complete with my stack of flyers.

Around this time, I really enjoyed listening to one morning radio show in Dallas. I thought both of the hosts were hysterical. It was the kind of show that as you kept listening to it, you felt like the hosts became friends. Another reason I liked it was that every Monday they had a psychic on to give readings to their listeners. She did not live in the Dallas area, but I knew her voice quite well. One morning, I heard that the station had fired their program director and the style of the show had changed. Their psychic was no longer part of the lineup.

I seized the opportunity and faxed them a letter explaining who I was—I now had some great clips to back me up. Until that moment, every piece of publicity I received had just come to me. This was the first time I had ever solicited an appearance on a program. I had never even seen a pitch for a show, so I truly had no idea what I was doing. But I was direct and to the point. I briefly stated that I was a practicing local psychic, that I was recognized as the Best Psychic in Dallas, and that I had appeared on local television a number of times. Within 2 hours of my sending the fax, the show's producer, Max, called me back.

"Hi, is this Dougall?" The radio voice echoed on my cell phone.

"Speaking."

"This is Max with the Daniel Meyerson show! We got your fax, and we are very interested in having you on our program."

"Wow, that's great!"

"I need to tell you up front that we can't pay you."

I had never even contemplated being paid—it just seemed like fun. I had certainly experienced the power of print and television, and I thought I would sample as many forms of media as I could. Actually, a big part of it was that I just wanted to meet Daniel and Judy, the hosts—especially Judy.

"I would never expect payment, Max. To be honest, I am a huge fan of the show and would be honored to be a guest."

He explained that I would be on the air the following Monday, and if things went well, they would have me on every week for a regular appearance. My heart stopped. This would be the perfect gig for me! It would be free advertising, and I would be a part of a show that was known for its humor. I loved doing the television spots, but there is only so much you can talk about in 4 minutes. On the radio, I would be on for over an hour!

The weekend before the show, I obsessed over what to wear to my meeting. I was trying things on in a local shop as the flustered saleswoman asked me what this was for.

"I am going to be on 789 the Jam tomorrow, and I must have the perfect outfit."

"But it's radio. No one is going to see it," she pointed out.

Well, yes, this is true, smarty pants, but still, any excuse for an outfit and I am all for it. I realize that selecting black flat-front pants over jeans is not going to help me connect to the other side, but it just makes me feel good. Most people dress for work every day—I didn't. And this was a big occasion.

The morning of the show, I did not even set my alarm. Who

could sleep? I turned the radio up to the highest volume so I could hear them talking before I got to the studio. There was no real mention of me, just that "a psychic" would be on later. When I got to the studio, I was a ball of nerves as it suddenly hit me that an hour was a very long time. (I had not taken into consideration that with commercial time and the other guests, I might get 15 minutes of airtime, if I was lucky. At the time, I was sure I was it for the full hour.)

In the lobby, I prayed, but this time I added a caveat to the prayer. It's normal for me to ask that information that is needed come through me, but this time I asked to have fun as well.

> **I realize that selecting black flat-front pants over jeans is not going to help me connect to the other side, but it just makes me feel good.**

Judy was a fairly well-known radio personality in the Dallas area. Her on-air persona was brazen and spunky. She had a laugh that caused one of two reactions: adoration or nausea. To me she was the Joan Rivers of Dallas. I knew who she was instantly when she came to the waiting room, stood in front of me, and asked, "Are you Doug?"

"I'm Dougall."

"Come this way."

"Are you Judy?" I asked politely.

"Yup."

Okey-dokey, someone did not have her happy pants on.

I had never been in a radio booth before. Their office was on one of the top floors of a Dallas high-rise building. On this foggy morning, you had to imagine what kind of view was behind the mask of gray. Judy walked up to a mike and sat down at a bar stool. Standing next to her was Daniel. My stomach was tied in knots.

"Thirty seconds," their producer announced.

Not much of a greeting as I was instructed to sit in this chair. I put on my earphones and heard the station's tagline, "The best of the '70s, '80s and '90s," in my ear.

"Dougall, can you count backward from 10 to 1?"

"One, 2, 3, 4, 5, 6, 7, 8, 9, 10!"

Now, this is the kind of behavior I just will never understand about myself. Would it have been that hard to count backward? No, I had to make a statement. I had to be cute and start from one. My dorky attempt at humor sailed right past everyone's head and fell flat on the floor. It only left me feeling like an idiot. Not the most auspicious beginning.

"Three seconds!" The producer called out.

"And we are back!"

I vaguely remember my introduction. There was certainly a shift as Judy suddenly went from unfriendly to very warm and playful. The dynamic duo were back, making fun of each other and making me feel at home. I was totally starstruck. I had been listening to this show for so long. I couldn't believe I was a part of this morning team, even if it was only for 15 minutes. (I found out later that this particular show that I loved so much had also recently been voted the Best of Dallas—best reason to turn off your radio.)

"Dougall Fraser is recognized as . . ." Blah, blah, blah.

During the interview, we joked back and forth with each other. That particular morning, I was on—funny, articulate, and noticeably vibing with Judy.

"When we come back, we will have Dougall give readings to our audience."

"Hey, Dougall, before we go to break, if people want to get a hold of you, what can they do?" Daniel asked. Great, a plug!

"They can call my office at—"

"You have an office! I don't have an *office!*" Daniel yelled.

"Psychics can have offices!" Judy defended me, and laughter ensued.

I leaned in to the mike and thought, *What the hell.* "Yeah, you can't miss it—there's a neon palm in the window."

Everyone laughed except Daniel. As we cut to commercial, I was feeling great.

Judy looked over at me and said, "You really are funny."

"Thanks!"

The program director came down and said, "You sound great on air. I'd like to get a reading afterward." By the end of the hour, I had read for the traffic guy and a bunch of listeners calling in. I felt more and more comfortable. The show turned out great—a perfect combination of chitchat and readings. I was home. After the show, I was taken into a board meeting and met some other people who worked on the program. I read for Judy, the program director, and a few other people on their team. Finally, Max came into the room. It was just the two of us. He smiled at me and asked if I would like to be a part of the show every week. I had died and gone to heaven.

"Dougall, are you gay?" Max asked.

"Yes, I am."

"We have a really big gay listening audience, and if you don't mind, we would love to have you be openly gay on air."

Of course! This was perfect. What wonderful people. I was so excited. For the next week, I told everyone I knew and happened to meet that I was now a part of the Daniel Meyerson morning show. Who cared that I wasn't being paid? I had received 80 calls the morning the show aired, but more importantly, I had had fun! I had asked for it, and I got it.

The Sunday night before my next appearance, my phone rang.

"Hey, Dougall, it's Max."

"Hi, Max, I can't wait for the show tomorrow! It's going to be great. I am so excited!"

"Listen, I hate to tell you this, but we have decided not to have you on tomorrow. We need to try some other things before we settle on one regular person again."

"Really?" Gulp. My heart sank.

"Don't worry. You'll be on again soon."

Well, one week became two, then three and four. During those times, they had some other psychics on the air. At first I was jealous, but then I thought, *Don't be greedy, Dougall. Think of all the fun the other psychics are having, just like you did.* But something felt wrong. My gut told me there was more to this story. My ego whined, *But I'm the Best Psychic in Dallas!*

A month after my appearance, I got a call from someone at the station. He told me what a great response they had had when I was on the air and that he thought I was really talented. But I would not be asked to appear on the show again.

"Really? Do you know why?"

"I'm not saying that this was said. But I think someone had a problem with you being gay."

I thanked him for the call and stared out the window. It had been so much fun. I had been myself. I didn't even say any-

I had come a long way to be happy and comfortable with myself; I wasn't going to compromise now.

thing about being gay—they asked me off the air. Maybe I shouldn't have been so honest. But that didn't feel like the right answer either. I had come a long way to be happy and comfortable with myself; I wasn't going to compromise now. Maybe I needed a different venue.

Chapter Ten

———◆◆———

TOO BIG FOR MY BRITCHES

MY CAREER AS A PSYCHIC HAD ENTERED A NEW TERRITORY: SMOOTH SAILING. I was making a very comfortable living in Dallas and, professionally speaking, was quite pleased with myself. I taught meditation classes, was booked at Above and Beyond any weekend I wanted to be, and had more private clients than I could handle. After the first time I was recognized in the grocery store, it started happening quite frequently, all over the place. In my own mind, I had become Catherine Zeta-Jones—I needed Jackie O sunglasses to enter any public space. Admittedly it was great fun, but I was not prepared for some of the drama that would ensue with becoming a marginal public figure.

One Saturday afternoon, I practically crawled into my car after my session at the gym. I had a trainer at the time, Steven, whom I secretly hated, though he tried to be a nice guy. He was just a meathead, but in a sweet kind of way. He used to ask about the man I was dating at the time by saying, "How's ya buddy?" I figured this was about as far as his straight mind could go. After an hour of torture, I made it to my car and could barely summon the strength to shift into reverse and drive home.

On the elevator ride up to my floor, I looked forward to spending the day alone, the thing I crave most on my days off. I spend my days counseling a number of people, and most of them are not in a good space. If you think about it, rarely does someone want to get a reading because they are engaged, just got a promotion, and are the happiest they have ever been. Ninety-five percent of the time, it's quite the opposite.

So Saturdays and Sundays are my days to just be. No candles, no incense, no one asking about a deceased relative. I live in the third dimension for 48 hours and love every minute of it. I watch MTV. I have brunch with Tarrin or friends. I shop. Whatever.

This Saturday, though, I stopped in my tracks as I reached for the doorknob to my loft. Something felt different. I wrapped my fingers around the cold metal and felt it slide right open. Why was the door not locked?

I slowly eased the door open, exposing the long rectangle of my loft apartment. From the front door, you could see all the way back, to a far wall of 10-foot-high windows. In the club chair in the designated living room area, facing the door, sat a stranger.

To me, the word "intruder" had always summoned up visions of a man dressed in black, with a ski mask (of course), maybe carrying a matching shoulder bag. He would rummage through the apartment, looking for "loot." This intruder was a well-dressed, middle-aged woman perched on my chair, designer handbag clutched in her hand. I gasped and jumped back in surprise.

"What the hell are you doing in here?"

"I have an appointment with you today," she said with annoying calm.

"That's impossible. I don't see clients on Saturdays."

"Why don't you work on Saturdays?"

"Because I don't have to. Wait, wait, wait. Why are we even discussing this? How the hell did you get inside my home?"

She stood up from the chair and started to approach me. I was prepared to enforce a karate chop if need be, but it was hard to feel threatened by a woman who was 20 years older than me and half my size. For the life of me, I could not imagine how she had gotten into my locked apartment. I was starting to feel very violated.

"There must be some misunderstanding. I thought I had my appointment today. Can we do the session anyway?" she asked in a conciliatory way.

"What is your name?"

She told me, and I said, "I think it's best that you leave right now." She wasn't getting her way, and she started to become angry with me.

"I need to speak with you today. I will pay you double."

Double? This was not a money issue. This was not about an appointment. This was about my privacy and boundaries. We had a very uncomfortable discussion. She begged me to read for her right that moment, and I told her that my energy did not feel clear. How could I counsel a woman who had invaded my space? (I try to make this clear to anyone whom I see—it is imperative that I know as little about you as possible before our session. I already knew way

She begged me to read for her right that moment, and I told her that my energy did not feel clear. How could I counsel a woman who had invaded my space?

too much about this woman—at the very least that she was spoiled
and selfish and would go to extremes to get what she wanted.)

I finally got her to leave, though she was very unhappy with my
decision. I sat down and pondered this new, unpleasant side of popularity. Now I had Suzy Q, an intruder and possible stalker,
claiming that the door had been left open. Even if that were true—
and it quite possibly could have been—a so-called unlocked door
does not give anyone carte blanche to enter my home. I was sure
that Suzy Q hadn't meant me any harm, but I was shaken by the
break-in.

This type of thing was happening more and more often. People
started showing up without appointments. Sometimes they were actual mistakes—2 instead of 5, or the 7th instead of the 17th. Those
things I understood, but the few times I actually found someone in
my home, I was livid. Their reaction was, How dare I be so rude? I
guess because my job title was "psychic," I was supposed to smile and
dance around when I opened the door and saw a stranger sitting in
my living room. "Oh, Suzy Q! I am so glad you are here. I can't wait
to read for you. Shall we sing a song together? Maybe I could make
you lunch!"

I'm not trying to sound ungrateful. The majority of the people that
I see, I am thrilled with. I enjoy the time we spend together, and that's
it. And I try to respect that with the people in my life, too. My therapist happens to work and, I assume, live in the same area as I do, the
Upper West Side of Manhattan. There are times when I see him on
the street. As much as I would like to believe that I am the most fascinating client that he has ever had, or that when he sees me at Zabar's,
he is dying to know how my week has been going, a gentle voice in my
head reminds me that he has a life outside of work. I always acknowledge him with a wave, a smile, whatever. But I don't show up at his
door unannounced during particularly bad weeks, and when I see him

in public, I do not stop him to update him on my life, however thrilling it may be.

Suzy Q and the others were not the norm. But after a few of these episodes, I did start to wonder about the safety of working in my home. Suzy Q hadn't really frightened me, physically. I was fairly positive I could protect myself from her. But several weeks later, my last appointment of the day was an interesting man.

It was a Thursday night, and I prepared for my 6:30 session. I was looking forward to the end of my workday. As I sat at my dining room table, I closed my eyes to get ready for Peter. The buzzer rang and security announced that I had a visitor, and I told the guard to send him up. A moment later, he knocked on my door.

"Hi, Peter, welcome. Please come in and sit at the table."

The moment Peter entered the apartment, chills ran up my back, the top of my head got very tingly, and I felt a little faint. Instantly I knew that I must be extremely cautious about whatever I said to this man.

I sat in my chair opposite him and tried to make eye contact. Peter was somewhere between the ages of 40 and 50. He had reddened skin from the outdoors, and his cologne permeated the air. By the sound of his accent, I guessed he was from Fort Worth. He placed his cash on the table, bills that were not quite as crisp as his starched shirt.

Keeping his eyes down, he mumbled, "I've been real excited to meet you."

"Well, Peter, it's a pleasure to have you here. Have I read for you before?"

"What—*don't you think you would remember me!*" he yelled. His fists were clenched, and he was suddenly furious. Something was seriously wrong with this man. The top of my head was now tingling so much, I was afraid I might pass out. I maintained eye contact with

As I picked up my tarot cards and began to shuffle them, I prayed in my mind. I called on Mary, Buddha, Wonder Woman, whomever. *Please, be with me now. I am not calm.*

this scary visitor as I debated how best to answer that question. Pete was much bigger than me. His eyes were not clear, and I could feel the anger in his chest.

"Peter, when I read for someone, I am in channel. Your name sounds familiar, and you even look familiar," I said with a gentle smile. "Why don't we begin?"

As I picked up my tarot cards and began to shuffle them, I prayed in my mind. I called on Mary, Buddha, Wonder Woman, whomever. *Please, be with me now. I am not calm.*

As I laid each card down, he interrupted me. Peter did not want a reading.

"Why is the FBI taping my phone conversations?" he asked me abruptly, over and over.

Peter moved through a 10-minute-or-so monologue about how the FBI was monitoring everything he said. He informed me that he was on disability, so he couldn't afford the computer program he needed to buy to remove the phone tap so they couldn't spy on him anymore.

I stayed silent. I listened intently, nodding with as much love and compassion pouring through my heart as possible. I knew he was probably a paranoid schizophrenic, and I also knew I was not trained to help Peter. It was not my job to tell him about mental illness and explain that the FBI was not tapping his phone line. In that moment, my only job was to keep him calm. At best, I could possibly inspire him to go to therapy.

"Well, Peter, if it is the FBI, which I can't quite tell, I am guessing they only want to make sure that you are okay. But I would assume that must be quite irritating for you."

"It is!" His shoulders hunched after that statement. He seemed calmer.

"This card means that you are really searching for answers right now," I continued. I am embarrassed to admit this. I did not give him much of a reading—I tried to calm him down. I spoke about a few minor things: his love of drawing, his ability to feel close to animals. Nothing that I would really consider to be psychic phenomena. I was looking into the eyes of someone lonely and ill. As we approached the end of the session, I made an attempt at the one thing I thought might really help him.

"Peter, I ask every person I see the same question at the end of a session. Have you ever thought of seeing a professional therapist?"

"Why the hell would I do that!" he screamed.

"Just curious. I do."

"Listen—the only reason I came here is because you are so damn cute. I bet the voices in your head are telling you not to have a date with me."

The tension in the room was making me so uncomfortable. I decided it was time to end the session.

"Peter, that is so kind of you. But I have a rule. I do not date clients. My belief is that if the universe brought you to me first as a client, then that is all our relationship can be."

Surprisingly Peter left without any problem. When the door closed behind him, I checked the lock at least a dozen times. Later that night, I had a message from Peter. He really wanted me to reconsider his invitation to dinner. Before I went to sleep, I prayed that God ask Peter to stay away from me and my home. He called incessantly for several weeks after that. His messages were all the same: "I

wish God would tell you what a nice guy I really am." I never returned any of the calls. My assistant alerted me that he was trying to
buy a ticket to a lecture I was giving—I had her call back and tell him
that it was sold out. I never saw Peter again, but added up, all these
incidents made an impression on me. I didn't think being "famous"
was quite so much fun anymore.

But PR was good for my business, so I listened when a friend called
me up and urged me to do another radio show. She was launching her
own publicity firm and decided she wanted to help me out.

"Dougall, I think you should go on 99.9," Kimyla proposed.

After my disaster with the Meyerson show, I was not too keen on
being on the radio again. "Twenty-two point five—that's alternative
music. Don't they cater to young kids?"

Something in my gut did not feel right about my appearing on
that station. As much as many psychics don't like to admit it, any appearance serves a twofold purpose. The first purpose, truthfully, is to
generate interest in my work and bring in clients. The second is to
help people. This station was not quite the right fit for me. Most
people that listened to it were in their late teens/early twenties—probably not the ideal audience of people looking to spend $100 on a
reading. But I decided that it might be fun. I told myself it was good
experience and I really shouldn't be concerned about how much
money I would make. Or not make.

"Okay, Kimyla," I said. "Give it a try."

We contacted the show, and I was booked. The week prior to my
appearance, I continued to have misgivings. I kept telling Kimyla over
and over that I wanted to cancel. She couldn't understand why.

"Dougall, it's good practice. It will be fun!"

Against a strong gut instinct, I decided to give radio in Dallas another go.

As I entered the building that housed the studio, I was more than nervous. Everything felt wrong. I was greeted by an intern at the reception area. He was a young kid—well, he was probably exactly my age, and that was young—dressed in a T-shirt boasting some band I had never heard of. Death by Dozens or Lady Bumble—something like that. I contemplated asking who the band was but decided that sounding like my father in that moment was not the way to start off.

He politely ushered me into the office. From the speakers on the wall, I could hear the show progressing until it was time for my segment.

My psychic radar screen was beeping a mile a minute. Sadly, even with my ability, I don't hear a booming voice that says: "Dougall, this is the universe talking. You need to leave this studio—I repeat—leave this studio."

I ignored the sensation and settled on the fact that I was just nervous.

"You're up," said the twerp.

I walked into the studio and was greeted by four people. The main host, Mitch, was a fairly famous guy. There were promo posters for his show all over the studio. He was quite handsome. We made eye contact, and the producer introduced me to the rest of the talent. I knew immediately that the female sidekick, Staci, would be the best person for me to read for. When our eyes met, she had a bright pink aura, an easy target. The other sidekick was somewhat lackluster. A nice guy, but he paid as little attention to me as I did to him.

The red light came on and Mitch said, "We are back on air. Dougall Fraser is here, and he is a psychic."

They started out by asking me a few questions and telling me that

My psychic radar screen was beeping a mile a minute. Sadly, even with my ability, I don't hear a booming voice that says: "Dougall, this is the universe talking. You need to leave—I repeat— leave now."

they did not believe in psychics at all. By this time, I was used to being on the radio or TV and not being treated very well at first. Especially on the radio. Typically a morning radio show host is somewhat of a glorified comedian. They have a great regular gig and love music. Psychics are not right up their alley. So I was prepared for them to make fun of my career; I laughed right along with them.

"So, prove you're psychic, Dougall," Mitch said challengingly.

I started with Staci. "Well, here is an example. When I look at Staci, I see pink surrounding her. Pink light is the light of perfection. Staci, you criticize yourself constantly. You are always picky. Nothing you ever do feels right."

When I said this, her eyes widened. Staci was an extremely attractive girl. You would never guess that she had body-image issues. As I confirmed this, she looked very interested in me.

"Well, that doesn't mean anything," Mitch interrupted. "I see *pink* triangles around Dougall!" Everyone started to laugh.

The pink triangle is a well-known gay-pride symbol. In retrospect, his comment, as far as content goes, was funny. I love a good joke. But this one hurt. I smiled anyway.

Sure, we were live on the air, but my friends weren't listening. It was no big deal anymore when I did a media appearance. In that moment, it was just me. While my entire being began to feel queasy, I tried to brush it off. We went to commercial.

The producer came in and noticed my discomfort. People who have never been on a radio show would be amazed at what goes on during commercial breaks.

"Look, now you are making the psychic upset," the producer said.

Mitch looked directly at me. He had extremely charming eyes. "Dougall, you are being a really good sport."

I felt deceived. But I nodded and tried to keep my focus.

"I wonder what it would feel like to fuck a skull," the producer suddenly blurted out. For the next 2 minutes, the crew, minus Staci, discussed their various hypotheses about what it would be like to fuck a skull. I was disgusted. Cutting-edge station or no, this was gross. I sat on my stool, with earphones on, ignoring them and hoping to God this interview would soon be over.

When the song ended, each host placed their headset back on, signaling that we were going back on the air.

"Dougall, I want you to prove to me that you are psychic," Mitch taunted me. I looked directly at him and saw small gold balls of light floating around his head.

"You have migraine headaches."

"Yes, I do. I've had them all my life."

"Well, I can see it in your aura."

"I'm not impressed. So what—you can see I have migraines?"

Everyone laughed. At that point, every psychic muscle in my being instantly atrophied. I could hardly hear what they were saying. Mitch's handsome eyes watched me tauntingly as he berated me over and over. I felt like I was 17 again. I happened to know that Mitch was gay. I happened to know that he was not out on the air. I also happened to have class. I refrained from outing him, though holding it back was killing me.

Mr. Lackluster chimed in. "What do you see about me?"

I was pretty much out of patience. "Fine. You really want me to read for you? You don't care what I say on air?"

"Yeah, you can't say anything about me that everyone doesn't already know!"

"You're married, right?"

"I am."

"I know that you talk about the girl you used to see before your wife so much that it drives her crazy. Every time you mention her name—which is way more than you should—she comments on it. You think about her all the time."

"Whoooaaaa!" Everyone in the studio was laughing. At least, for a moment, not at me but at him. It really was high school again: getting the bullies to laugh at someone else besides me, if only for a moment.

"He so does!"

There is a good reason I don't like to read for the hosts on the air: They have a public persona that they would like to keep. I respect that. I'm on their territory, so I do my best to demonstrate my work without divulging anything too personal. But I had been pushed, and I was feeling cornered.

Mitch asked if we could take some calls. I agreed, hoping to God the show would just end as soon as possible.

"First caller, do you have a question for Dougall?"

"Yeah, Dougall, can you tell what race I am?" he snickered.

"That's a funny one."

As I spoke to the callers one by one, all of whom had only joke questions for me, I heard Indian music in my earphones.

"How do you like your theme music, Dougall?" Mitch asked.

"I like it. That's funny." And it really was funny.

"Well, I think *this* should be your theme music!"

Mitch flipped a switch, and suddenly Abba's "Dancing Queen" burst through the airwaves at full blast. They all cracked up. I did not. In fact, I was no longer in the room. My body remained in my stool with headphones on, but my soul was somewhere else. The best little psychic in Dallas was not being treated too well. I was prepared to be made fun of for my job, but I was not prepared to be made fun of for being gay. Actually, I had not been made fun of for being gay in quite some time. My heart sank. The radio interview was over.

When I got back into my car, I quickly turned to 99.9.

They were finishing an interview with a writer from a magazine like *Rolling Stone*. As they hung up with the phone interview, Mitch said, "What a weird day. We had the gay writer and the gay psychic." Everyone laughed, and I drove home feeling awful.

I could not get Mitch's cruelty out of my mind. *"You're being a good sport"* played over and over in my head. Maybe I was too sensitive, but I was really hurt. Why is it that in moments like that, it's only later we come up with the perfect things we could have said?

I spent the rest of the morning ashamed of my behavior. I hadn't defended myself. I was chubby Dougall in high school again. I needed to fix the situation. So I called GLAAD—the Gay and Lesbian Association Against Defamation. I left them a message.

"Yes, this is Psychic Dougall Fraser, and I just appeared on a radio show. . . ."

I ran through the entire humiliating event. I was sure a press conference would be scheduled immediately. Rosie O'Donnell would run to my rescue. I would have hot male lawyers at my side, telling me everything was going to be okay. Mitch would be forced to apologize. I soothed my hurt pride with these visions

Why is it that in moments like that, it's only later we come up with the perfect things we could have said?

for a day or two. Long story short, GLAAD never returned my phone call.

The next week, I picked up a copy of the *Dallas Voice*, the local gay rag. They had an article about 99.9 and its morning crew that said that a number of times, the crew had made some antigay remarks. Even though I'd experienced it firsthand, I was still shocked. I did not understand how a gay host could do that. It was his choice to remain closeted, but that didn't mean that you could make fun of someone else just to get the eyes off you.

My confidence was shaken. I was certainly not as high on Dallas as I had been. I felt like I had done it all, saturated the market. I was certain there was a more sophisticated market out there somewhere, where things like that radio interview just wouldn't happen.

AFTER THE RADIO APPEARANCE, THE THOUGHT OF LEAVING DALLAS ENTERED MY MIND. I was mulling over my options when I received an offer to read at a private black-tie function.

I don't really like reading at parties. I always tell people who want to hire me: If you want me to do readings for people in a party setting, you need to have a list, you need to be prepared that someone will leave, and there will certainly end up being an argument. No one ever listens. "Not my friends—we all get along so well. . . ."

This party was no different. I didn't really want to do it, but they offered me such a big fee that I couldn't say no. After the latest radio debacle, my self-esteem was still a work in progress—I probably would have done it for a Diet Coke and a bucket of KFC.

There were 700 people at the party, so many that they had hired two psychics to read for all the guests. I was being paid a lot of money to be there, and no one was stopping by my table. The palm reader was sitting there, too, just as bored as I was. So I got up and mingled. I walked through the party and did a few quick readings for people, just passing by. I kept them fun and light, like "You must be self-employed." "I am self-employed—wow!"

Pretty soon people started coming over and sitting down. By the end of an hour, I'd done four or five readings, and I had a line of 15 people impatiently waiting their turn to get to me. I put up a list, which is the only way to handle things because you would not believe how so-called adults act when someone cuts the line. "Hey, why does she get to go first? I was supposed to get my reading first!"

This gala fund-raiser was being attended by some of the wealthiest people in Dallas, which, in the land of oil, is saying something. Sometimes, at events like these, where it's loud and there are hundreds of people milling around and drinking and smoking everywhere, I might ask for a ring or a watch to do some psychometry to help me focus. At the end of the night, my 4-hour block of time was done, and I was packing up my stuff getting ready to go. There was still a line of more than 50 people waiting to see me, and they got really upset. "Hey, we still want readings!"

I said, "I'm really sorry. My time is up."

I just didn't like the way they were treating me. One of the women in charge said, "Well, can we just come to your office this week?"

"Actually, I'm booked about 4 months in advance. If you'll contact my assistant, she'll make the first available appointment for you."

"Oh, really?" in the full-on Texas drawl. "Well, Ah might just have to hire you for a li'l party. How much would it be to hire you for a party, darlin'?" I was a little paid monkey who had to dance to her tune.

> It wasn't about the money; I didn't need their money or them. This was a contest of wills, and I lost.

"Come on, honey. Stay for just 1 more hour. Name yoh price. Everybody got a price."

It wasn't about the money; I was 21 years old, making almost six figures. I didn't need their money or them. This was a contest of wills, and I lost. I was just too young and inexperienced. This was a middle-aged Dallas socialite wearing probably $500,000 worth of jewelry, and she was used to getting her way. She smiled indulgently at me. "In't he cute? Come on, darlin.' How much?"

"Fine, for $200 I'll stay for a half-hour longer." I thought for sure she would say no. She didn't bat an eye. "Fahn, $200. Just set raght back down."

So I unloaded my stuff and sat back down. I couldn't believe I was whoring myself out for $200, but it happened to be my car payment, so I said to myself, *Fine. It's 30 minutes. Who wouldn't do it?* I did one reading, and then it was the woman's turn. She had a wad of cash in her hand. She dropped in on the table, then turned around and told her friends, "Ah just paid him two hunnerd dollars." Turning back to me, "Ah *own* you for 30 minutes."

At that moment, I swore to myself I would never do another party. If I wasn't going to whore for the psychic hotline, I certainly wasn't going to be the whipping boy for these people. I knew it was time to leave Dallas and live on a different level.

Chapter Eleven

IF I CAN MAKE IT THERE . . .

THE LITTLE VOICE IN MY HEAD TELLING ME IT WAS TIME TO LEAVE
DALLAS BECAME IMPOSSIBLE TO IGNORE. I loved Dallas (still do), but
I wanted diversity. I wanted to live in a city where being gay was as
normal as being straight, and though Dallas was wonderful in many
ways, that it would never be. My friend Kerry had landed a job in the
Bay Area and rhapsodized about the California life. I decided I would
move to either San Francisco or New York City.

Whenever a client has asked me what city to move to or where I
see them living, I approach their question from two different angles.
First, I make a "blind" prediction as to where I see them. Second, we
discuss the cities or areas that they feel drawn to. If I am correct, that's
great. If I am not correct, no big deal. I tell them, "Test me, but go to
the places that you feel pulling you toward them. Feel the energy
of the land. See if you connect with the topography and the climate
and the people of that area."

Deciding where I would live next gave me a great opportunity to
follow my own advice. Seeing as I grew up outside of New York City,
I knew what that city's vibe was for me. San Francisco, however, was

Deciding where I would live next gave me a great opportunity to follow my own advice.

foreign territory. I booked a trip to go out and test the waters.

San Francisco is a stunningly beautiful city. As I walked the streets, I felt as though I were strolling through a movie set. The architecture was completely new to me, and I loved the combination of urban bustle blanketed over a mountainous terrain. Not to mention that as a gay man, I was in the Mecca for Our People. It certainly provided a sense of acceptance. From the moment I had boarded the plane—where I looked at my fellow passengers and decided that every other passenger on my flight was gay—I was in the heart of gay-pride land.

Kerry set up some sessions for me to do, so I had some work during my trip, and I stayed in a hotel, explored the city, and made an attempt to find housing. Every appointment I made to see an apartment or to meet with a real estate agent failed miserably. I would show up at the wrong address. I would find the right location, but the landlord wouldn't make it. It was extremely frustrating. I loved the City by the Bay; it felt like home. I truly wanted to be there. But the universe was speaking to me, and I was not listening.

The following month, I went back to New York to see my family. In the years since I'd moved away, we had all started to meet every summer at my grandmother's home in Cutchogue, New York. Cutchogue is somewhat of a secret in Long Island. During the summer, everyone from the city bolts to the Hamptons. They hobnob with the stars and dine in fancy-schmancy restaurants. If you have never been to the Hamptons, it is truly something to see. Admittedly, however, it has lost much of its "country charm." Now instead of farmer's markets, there are traffic and trendy boutiques.

On the opposite side of the island is where my family has a home. Cutchogue still has a "local" vibe. The streets are lined with farm stands. The Prada flip-flops of the Hamptons transform into Filene's Basement flip-flops on the North Fork.

As we gathered in Cutchogue that summer, I told my dad that I was ready to leave Dallas and was seriously contemplating moving to California. My dad considered this. He loves to give business advice. His wisdom to me was a combination of great business savvy and a small dose of self-service.

"Well, Sport . . .," he started, and I was immediately transported back to childhood. When I was a kid, I won the trophy for star couch potato, but my father's favorite nickname for me was always "Sport." As I would leave for school, he would say from his chair, "Challenge yourself, Sport!" For years, this was like nails on a chalkboard to me. Depending on the situation, Sport would be replaced by various other titles—sometimes I was "Ipso-Facto" or "Mr. Big Stuff." To this day, I am still a bit partial to "Champ."

"Let's talk," he continued, and we got down to brass tacks.

I explained to my dad my reasons for wanting to leave Dallas. If I was going to take my career to the next level, I needed a state with a bigger city. California was my favorite option. He gave me his thoughts.

"You are going to pay at least double in rent in San Francisco, Champ."

Wasn't that the truth. Looking at apartments there had thrown me into sticker shock. "I know, but I think many of my clients will do phone readings, and it probably won't be too hard to get exposure there."

"Ya think so, Sport? You will also need your car there."

"True. I had also thought of moving to New York, to live in the city."

After running through some general numbers, we decided it would cost at least $2,500 to move my furniture to California. Plus, I would need money for security, first and last month's rent, and a car and insurance. It was going to take a lot of effort. Though I had been making good money for a while now, saving was not and will never be one of my strengths. (We all have issues, and this is one of mine.) The bottom line was, though I made a very decent living in Dallas, I had nothing to show for it.

"I'll make you an offer, Sport—if you move to New York, I'll pay for the movers."

It was a generous offer. In Manhattan, I wouldn't need a car. I could stay at my father's in Garden City until I found proper housing in the city. It seemed like a good sign. I have to admit, Dad knew how to close a deal.

I returned to Dallas and made up my mind that I was moving back to New York. My lease on the loft happened to be ending in November of 1999, so I moved into Tarrin's house for the last 2 months of the year to save some moving money. Or at least that was the goal. I set my sights on moving to New York during the first week of January 2000. A new millennium, a new life.

I went into overdrive. I packed all my things and sent them ahead to my dad's house in New York. I moved into the house Tarrin shared with her husband, Bill, and decided to rent space from Above and Beyond. My schedule quickly filled up with people eager for one more reading in person before I left town.

One day, as I prepared for another fully booked day at Above and Beyond—seven back-to-back appointments—I realized I had left my tarot cards at home and freaked out. I had never done a full private reading without my cards, and I was panicked. I had carried my bag with the cards with me everywhere since I was 12 years old. I didn't necessarily always use them, but I always had them near so I could hold them. I felt secure knowing they were within reach. My cards were to me what that blanket was to Linus.

The whole tarot card or crystal thing is fascinating to me. I now think it goes back to people's not wanting to take responsibility for themselves. I think it went all the way back to my childhood for me. I hadn't wanted to believe that I was psychic myself; I wanted to believe that it was coming from somewhere else, so I read cards obsessively. It was much easier for me to say to someone: "You have financial problems because that's what this card says" or "You're lazy. . . . *I'm* not saying that, but that's what the card is telling me."

When my first client of the day sat down across from me, I said, "Listen, I don't have my cards. Now, I want to be completely honest with you. I've never done this before, but I'm just going to go with it." And my reading was incredible; in fact, all my readings kicked butt that day. They were better than usual because I wasn't letting anything get in the way. I wasn't sitting there thinking, *That card has a tree on it and that one has a peacock and that one has a horse, so maybe that means they like animals.* I was just in the flow, and it was the first time that I confidently just went full steam ahead and read. Same bike, just no training wheels.

> **I hadn't wanted to believe that I was psychic myself; I wanted to believe that it was coming from somewhere else, so I read tarot cards obsessively.**

Was the experience any different for my clients? Probably not—

in fact, if anything, they got a better reading. That day it was all about honoring my power. I was the one doing it; I was the vessel. It was very scary but very liberating.

I remembered reading once for a very renowned card reader, someone who had studied the cards for years, down to the tiniest detail. She was schooled in all the various decks and every nuance possible. And after her reading, she told me, "Dougall, I don't know what you're doing with those, but whatever it is, keep it up because it works." I didn't even do a proper spread. I just liked to lay them out because they looked cool. This woman said, "That is so not what that card means, but that was a damn good reading, so don't worry about it."

Look, if someone gives you a reading and tells you the cards don't lie, that's just not true. The cards lie all the time! Ouija boards lie, pendulums lie, and cards lie. The Bible lies! These are not living things. People are always looking for this one great, all-knowing tool.

Think about it: If Tarot cards were 100 percent accurate, what kind of life would we lead? Part of being a human being is waiting for good news. When you were a child, did you ever search your house for your hidden Christmas gifts? I have, and that was one of the more disappointing Christmas mornings of my life because there was no surprise. Sure, we would all like to be shielded from pain, but we can't ask a person or a card—or a board game, for that matter—to give us all the answers. The universe is not a physical item!

> **Look, if someone gives you a reading and tells you the cards don't lie, that's just not true. The cards lie all the time!**

To this day, especially if I'm doing a radio show, I bring my cards with me and spread them out. I like to have them near, even though I don't have a clue what any of them mean. But I think many of us get too attached to astrology and tarot cards and dream catchers and angel spirit cards, when the truth of the matter is that what we are seeking is a connection to the divine.

That day was a turning point; I had found my connection to the divine and never doubted my powers again. I still carried my cards, but I didn't use them much anymore.

I packed them in for the rest of my time in Dallas.

My television appearances had given me a boost. My regular clients were anxious to see me in person before I left, and everyone wanted to hear what was coming up in the new millennium. I was frantically busy, doing readings from morning to night. The final weeks raced by.

Picture it: New Year's Eve 1999. A bunch of gay men get together for the celebration of the millennium. I have never been much of a fan of New Year's Eve; it falls into the same category as Valentine's Day. I always feel enormous pressure to have the best night of my life. That thought was exaggerated quite a bit for December 31, 1999. It would be one of my last nights in Dallas.

Originally I planned to attend a silent retreat somewhere. I wanted to enter the new millennium in an atmosphere of peace and serenity. I had the fantasy of a gorgeous retreat in a mini-mansion sitting high atop a hill. Each private room would have a small bed, a beanbag chair, and a terrace that overlooked the lake. I would eat vegetarian cuisine and spend the day listening to harp music. I would wear robes and reflect on the momentous turn of the century and spiritually prepare myself for my new life.

I had searched and searched on the internet for a Buddhist

monastery where I could stay for several days. There were none. So I looked instead for any kind of New Year's workshop that was more spiritually based than celebration-based. There were exactly none, as far as I could tell. The rest of the world wanted to party like it was 1999.

"Dougall, are you ready yet?" Jeremy called impatiently.

The night of New Year's Eve found me in my friend Jeremy's bathroom trying to fix my hair, preparing for the exact opposite of my fantasy. There would be no monks at this party. The only similarity between this night and my fantasy was that I would be surrounded exclusively by men.

We would all like to be shielded from pain, but we can't ask a person or a card—or a board game, for that matter—to give us all the answers.

That night, our large group went to Cedar Springs. Besides celebrating the year 2000, the gathering was somewhat of my last hurrah. I don't recall the evening as being too special. I drank too much; I kissed more than my fair share of toads. At 4 A.M., we decided to call it a night—or morning, as was the case. I stumbled out of the club, surrounded by the people in Dallas that I called friends. As we walked up the street to catch a cab, I looked down and caught a glimpse of my face under my friend's boot.

"John, look—you just walked all over me!"

"What?"

"You just stepped on me—look."

He stopped, and we both looked at the newspaper caught under his heel. My face beamed out from the cover of the *Dallas Voice*.

"No Armageddon in 2000, Psychic Says," read the headline.

This was my interview with the local gay paper that had come on the heels of my disastrous radio show appearance. Their interview with a psychic was timed to come out the last week of December so I could make predictions for the new millennium. It had been all over the city the past few days. This piece in the *Voice* was the first time a prediction I made appeared in print. Underneath my picture, the copy continued. (Of course, they misspelled my name.)

> Gay psychic Dougal Fraiser says new millennium won't bring disaster, unless you count President George W. Bush. . . . The openly gay psychic says 2000 will see a rush of celebrities coming out of the closet, a win by Hillary Clinton in New York and significant new progress in the medical battle against AIDS."

I had come to Dallas to find myself, and just as I was leaving, I got such a powerful validation of how far I had come. I looked handsome in the picture. I did not feel the need to criticize my body. Sure, I was nervous that I had made predictions that might not come true, but much more importantly, I was me. I was the feature story in a gay paper. I was very far from the chubby high school dropout studying massage. I was making good money and had a good reputation. And on New Year's Eve, I was not sitting in a silence retreat. I was out with my friends, laughing about it. In my heart, I knew I had accomplished what I needed to do. Dallas had done its job.

MANHATTAN HAS BUZZ AND EXCITEMENT AND ENERGY LIKE NO OTHER PLACE ON EARTH. As I deplaned, the sound of familiar accents all around me reminded me that I was back in New York. The city has a pulse, and I could feel it the moment I started walking through the airport. As I stood waiting for my luggage at the baggage carousel, my phone rang.

"Hi, Dougall, this is Maggie calling from the *Queen Latifah Show*."

I was stunned. At this point, Queen Latifah was hosting a nationally syndicated daytime talk show.

"We are interested in possibly having you on our show."

I had been in New York for less than 30 minutes, and I got a call from a national talk show! My heart was pounding. It felt as though the pulse of the city were matching the pulse and rhythm of my own body. We were in sync. Maggie asked me to send her a head shot and demo tape of my work. Surely this was a very clear sign I had made the right choice in coming back to New York.

From the airport, I planned to go to my friend Beth's apartment and stay with her in the city for the weekend. Beth had offered to help me find an apartment in New York. I had never seen her place before, but I knew she was paying a little less than what I had paid for my loft apartment in Dallas. I imagined a sophisticated urban apartment, Beth and me strolling the streets having lattes at sidewalk cafés, checking out beautiful prewar apartment buildings.

Even though I had grown up on Long Island—just 30 minutes outside of Manhattan—we never came to the city. A lot of the kids in my neighborhood didn't, though their fathers might commute from Garden City to work each day. New York City was as foreign to me as Alaska. Everyone in Dallas kept saying, "Well, you're moving home," which geographically, I guess, was true. But I wasn't going to Garden City. I was in the big city now, and I was clueless.

I did not know my way around Manhattan at all. From the airport, I took the Long Island Rail Road (LIRR) to Penn Station. It was totally foreign territory. I was in the midst of a huge crowd of people racing around, and I had no idea what to do. What had I gotten myself into? I found the nearest exit and raced out. It was January 15, and the freezing air hit me in the face. The ground was covered in snow. Coming from Dallas, I was not prepared for a northern winter. I had no hat (I typically opt for good hair over warmth) and no gloves.

I hailed a cab—well, actually, I hailed a Lincoln. Everyone is familiar with the yellow cabs of New York City, but on this particular day, a black Lincoln Town Car pulled up to the corner. A lovely man asked in a friendly voice where I was headed. I had been repeating Beth's address in my head over and over and over: *Twenty-fifth between Second and Third. Twenty-fifth between Second and Third.* It was so important that I know what I was doing.

My first mistake was not jumping in a yellow cab. But I really thought that this limo driver saw me trying to hail a yellow cab and thought, *That poor young socialite shouldn't be in a common car—I'll pick him up.* The limo driver was a nice guy. As I settled myself in the backseat, he asked, "You visiting?"

"Yes, well, actually I just moved here." After my years in Dallas, I had a Southern twang in my voice.

Before I could finish answering the question, he swerved his way into traffic, heading in a direction I now know was completely wrong. My bag flew off the seat and hit the floor. As horns blared and cars whizzed by, I grabbed my bag and held on to it with white knuckles, trying to project an image of calm and complete comfort.

When we arrived at Twenty-fifth between Second and Third, he informed me that the fare was $15. I now know that a yellow legal cab would have cost me maybe $5—including tip. The driver of the

Lincoln—or gypsy cab, as they are called—was not supposed to randomly pick people up. But he saw an idiot without a hat on and knew. I paid the fare—I didn't know any better.

In 2000 in Dallas, $800 a month would get you a decent apartment—one with a security gate, a pool in the complex, and a parking spot. A perfectly fine, good-size one-bedroom in a nice neighborhood. I immediately realized that $800 a month in New York was a whole other story. Beth lived in a sixth-floor walk-up. I was disgusted by the stairwell in the building; it looked as though it hadn't been cleaned in months. I was sure I would find an apartment for around $1,200 in a much better building.

Finally, after hauling my bags up six flights in a dark, dirty stairwell, I reached Beth's apartment. When she opened the door and invited me to step inside, the look on my face must have been classic. I was standing inside the smallest apartment I had ever seen in my life. The kitchen was the size of my bathroom in Dallas. Her bathroom was minuscule. I could shower, pee, and brush my teeth at the sink, all at the same time. Just getting in the shower stall was like a scene from Cirque de Soleil. I looked around myself in shock.

"You pay $800 a month for this? And why is it so freakin' hot in here?"

"Dougall, I'm *lucky* to live here! This is considered a one-bedroom apartment! It's really cheap. It's hot because I can't control the heat."

It was the dead of a bitterly cold winter. Snow was falling outside, and all of Beth's windows were wide-open. It was still at least 80 degrees in the tiny apartment.

"Well, I'm sure I'll find something bigger."

Beth was very sweet. She explained to me that it had taken her a long time—months—to find this palace and that I should probably expect to look for about a year before I settled on a place to live.

That seemed absurd. In my mind, I was just about to appear on the *Queen Latifah Show*. I had conquered Dallas, after all. I was going to be just fine.

Chapter Twelve

NEW YORK CHARM

AFTER MY WEEKEND IN THE CITY, WITH BETH PLAYING TOUR GUIDE, I RETURNED TO MY FATHER'S HOME IN GARDEN CITY. In the back of my mind, I'd had a little New York fantasy about how fun it would be to live with a friend for a few weeks, just until I found suitable housing. After only 2 days, I realized this was not an option. We were packed in like sardines in Beth's apartment. Also, I was just not limber enough for the bathroom.

I went back to my roots: staying with Dad. My mother had also returned to her roots; she had moved to Rochester to be near her family. Jorge accompanied her; but sadly, he died shortly after they arrived. My childhood home had been sold to another family, but Dad lived only 5 minutes away from my old house. I truly had come home again—and I was determined not to stay.

I decided I needed to get moving and set myself some small goals. My immediate concern was to find a workplace. My father offered to let me start out in his building on Long Island, but even free rent was not tempting enough to keep me away from the city. So I set off to find my office.

I contacted a local acupuncture school and posted a listing in their common area saying I was looking to share space with someone in a similar field. Within 24 hours, I received a call. A chiropractor studying at the school had an office on Seventeenth Street, and she had a room to rent out. I took this as another sign, a most promising one.

Monday morning, I woke up and prepared to look at this potential space. I walked from my father's home to the LIRR. It was like being in a time machine; walking the familiar streets of Garden City was very eerie. The sense of being an imposter still remained, but there was a different edge this time to my stride. I was now glad to be an outsider. Being different was a conscious choice. I was rejecting suburbia; suburbia was not rejecting me.

The sense of being an imposter still remained, but there was a different edge this time to my stride. I was now glad to be an outsider.

I found the chiropractic office on Seventeenth Street, in Chelsea. (I was getting a bit better at the navigation business.) It was a nondescript 10-story building, one you could easily walk right by. As soon as the elevator door opened onto the 10th floor, I knew I had found the right place. I walked into a common reception area and looked around. The whole space was easily 2,000 square feet. It had very high ceilings, large windows, and an "earthy" feeling about it. Darleen, the owner, and I sat down to discuss rent. To rent a room that was smaller than my walk-in closet in Dallas was going to cost more each month than what I had paid for the entire loft. By now, I knew that looking around for a better deal wasn't even an option; this *was* a good deal, and I liked the feel of the place. I took a deep breath and handed over a check for the deposit. I realized that once I got some furniture moved in, my so-called savings would be gone. It was a panicky feeling. But I had an address in New York City. I had fulfilled my first goal.

Every day I went into my new office eager to work, but the phones were not ringing. I had a few clients in Dallas who continued to book phone appointments, but not many. I was used to being booked solid at least 3 weeks (if not months!) in advance. Self-promotion had no longer been an issue; I had created a thriving practice.

As I sat in my new New York City office, I would stare out the window at a lovely view of another window. The sounds of the city started to feel like laughter—at me, not with me. Had I made a horrible mistake? Staring at my new phone system, which cost more than I would like to admit, I waited for the red light to ignite. Every day I reassured myself that it had taken me quite some time to make a mark in Dallas, and I should expect it to take just as much time here. *If I build it, they will come. . . .*

I spent most of my workdays sitting at my desk and brainstorming ways to get exposure. I went to local New Age bookstores and health food stores to pick up their free magazines. As time passed and nothing much happened businesswise, I knew I could always contact one of the psychic fairs in the city, but I just could not bring myself to make the call. Once I'd become a fixture on the Dallas circuit, I realized how exhausting and unfulfilling those fairs could be. I had worked so hard to leave that part of the community behind. No, I wouldn't do that again. I'd had some clout in Dallas; I'd made a name for myself—surely it was only a matter of time before I'd break out in New York.

To begin, I thought I should make contact with some of the other psychics in the greater New York area. In Dallas, I had a number of other psychics that I referred people to, so I thought it would be a good and logical idea to talk with the locals. I quickly found out this was not a very common practice.

I had heard of a man that worked as a medium on the Upper East Side. He was fairly well-known, and from what some friends had told me, he was very good.

"Hi, is this Mark?"

"Yes, it is."

"Hi, Mark, my name is Dougall Fraser. I am a psychic. I just moved to the city and am looking to make some contacts. I thought maybe I could refer people to you, or you could give me some pointers on places to get—"

"No, I'm not interested." Click.

Most people were not that harsh—many just humored me on the phone for a couple of minutes and wound up the conversation by saying they didn't ever refer their clients to other psychics. This wasn't the first time that I had seen this kind of attitude, but it still surprised me.

I don't know—maybe all other psychics in the country are able to meet all of their clients' needs. For me, personally, that has never been the case. A perfect example is someone I have been giving readings to for a long time. If I get to know a person, meaning that they come back to me for a second, third, or even fourth session, I start to care about them personally. I become biased. For me to be as accurate as possible, it is best for me not to remember or know anything about my clients. That way, I am looking at all of their life situations from a neutral place. In Dallas, if I knew a lot about someone and my energy didn't feel clear, I had no problem sending "my" client to someone else for a reading. It seemed only reasonable to me.

After a couple weeks of trying to connect with the psychic community of New York—and not getting very far—I decided maybe I should try to get back on TV. Publicity was what I needed, so I created a press release on my computer.

"Psychic Dougall Fraser Now Lives in New York!" the headline read in great big, bold type. Okay, don't laugh—I truly thought someone might recognize my name. At this point, my largest exposure had been appearing on the Texas morning shows, but you never know. I faxed all the local TV stations, *alerting* them to my arrival. Explaining that I had plenty of television experience and was available for appearances. And then I waited for my phone to ring. And waited, and waited some more.

> **For me to be accurate, it's best for me not to remember or know anything about my clients.**

At this point, John Edward was the Ricky Martin of the psychic world. People were mesmerized by him, as they should be. John Edward is by far one of the most talented mediums of our world. I, however, am not a medium. I repeat: I am not a medium. And that was about to cost me the appearance on *Queen Latifah*.

"Hi, Dougall, it's Maggie from the *Queen Latifah Show.*"

"Hi, Maggie, good to hear from you. Did you get my demo tape?"

"We sure did, and it looks great. Quick question, Dougall—can you contact dead people?"

This would be the first of many times I would hear that question. The *Queen Latifah Show* wanted to do a segment very similar to *Crossing Over*, John Edward's wildly popular show where he contacted friends and family members on the other side for his audience.

Unfortunately, that's just not something I do. I tried to explain that I was more of a psychic life coach.

"Maggie, I don't talk to dead people. Think of me as the psychic that talks to the living! I focus on lifestyle issues. Like finding love, prosperity, and spiritual happiness. How to live your best life."

Maggie seemed intrigued, but I never heard from her again. My heart was broken. Not only was my *Queen Latifah* dream gone, but the local shows were not calling me at all.

I dragged home from a long, boring day at the office. I had done one reading for a former client in Dallas and spent the rest of the day shuffling papers in the hopes that I would appear very busy. When I opened the door, I was accosted by Father's new children, his dogs. I was stressed, first from living at home again and now having a teenage basset hound lunging at me.

"Hey, Sport, how was your day?"

I had only been home about a month, and yet the sound of my father's voice catapulted me back to adolescence. Before I could respond, I had to remind myself that I was an adult, I think.

"Well, Dad, it's tough. Not much activity yet."

"Maybe you should get a part-time job in sales, kiddo."

"Maybe I need a drink."

My dad thinks the secret to success is sales. For him I suppose that is true—he is a very successful man and an admirable salesperson. Our approaches to our respective careers are different. In Dallas, when my business had been booming, he'd suggested I try to find other psychics to work in my office. "That's how you make more money, kiddo," he'd assured me. For him it was true, but in my world, I was not looking to become some kind of ESP conglomerate. I just wanted to help people.

"Maybe you should start advertising." The ice in my dad's scotch clinked as he suggested this idea.

"Dad, psychics don't advertise. In my business, it's word of mouth."

For me this had been true. I had tried advertising before but really had no response. I had built an entire career on referrals. I had a hard time believing it could be any different.

"What if for a year I paid for advertising and we will see how it goes?"

"Dad, I really, really don't want to advertise."

"You are so stubborn—just try it!"

For a moment something clicked. Maybe I was being too stubborn. I was always telling clients to get the energy moving. I suggest making new business cards, creating flyers, a newsletter—anything to show the universe that you are trying to create income. It's a basic spiritual principle: Energy follows thought, and thought directs energy. In essence, my placing an ad for my work would be a tangible form of the law of attraction. I decided to let my dad pay for it for a year—wasn't that nice of me?

The first week the ad ran, I booked 10 appointments. One Monday morning, my first session was with Allison. She was the very first reading in New York I'd booked from my advertisement. I was thrilled.

"Hi, Allison, I'm Dougall."

"I am so glad I saw your ad. I had no idea how to find a psychic, and I have been wanting to get a reading for a really long time. I am a little nervous."

Allison was an attractive young black woman. She couldn't have been taller than 5'0". As I briefly explained the process of a session, her eyes wandered past me and examined my office—which didn't take too long.

> I was always telling clients to get the energy moving. It's a basic spiritual principle: Energy follows thought, and thought directs energy.

"Are you ready, Allison?"

"Oh, sorry, yes."

She took a deep breath and closed her eyes as if to show me that she took this very seriously.

"Allison, it feels like you just lost your job, but I am happy about that, for some reason. It seems like a good thing." Her eyes were still closed. "You can open your eyes, Allison."

She opened them and looked right at me. "I did just lose my job, sort of."

"Have you ever thought of being a hairdresser?"

"I am a hairdresser!" she laughed.

Those first 10 clients turned into 15, and on and on it went. It was a perfect lesson in the proven point that the universe delivers abundance in a variety of ways. I was so busy sitting at my desk, staring at the phone and waiting. I was pulling every spiritual card I knew: I envisioned a thriving practice, I lighted candles, I prayed, I was getting ready to sacrifice a chicken. In my mind, I was the successful psychic who had made it and no longer needed to work at creating abundance in my life. Not true. I had forgotten to keep the ball rolling. I had not done anything tangible. As I tell clients over and over, the universe wants to see effort; it will return your energy tenfold. In that moment, my father became my teacher, or my angel, so to speak. I had to remove my stubbornness because it was standing in the way of my success.

Now that I was getting on my feet, I started hunting for a new home. My father's house was only an hour door-to-door from my office—certainly not a bad commute—but I didn't like being a slave to public transportation; it took a lot of getting used to. I love to drive. A car gave me the illusion of being in control of my life. If I wanted to speed, I could; if I wanted to take the scenic route, I could. That was not an option on the subway. *Um, I'm going to 14th Street, so can't we just skip 34th, 28th, 23rd, and 18th?* No, in New York, we were all in it together.

Cabs became my temptation. Money was bleeding steadily out of my savings account as I opted to pay $15 for a cab ride versus $1.50 for the subway. Every morning by the time I arrived at the office, I had already spent $20 just in transportation.

Every Wednesday, I picked up a copy of the *Village Voice* to look at listings for available apartments. In Dallas, looking for an apartment had been a really delightful experience. When you entered the rental office of the complex, you were seated in a model living room. Many times the scent of freshly baked cookies wafted in from the model kitchen. You were offered coffee or tea or a soda before a busty young thing asked, "What kind of apartment home are y'all lookin' for?"

The universe wants to see effort, and it will return your energy tenfold. I had to remove my stubbornness because it was standing in the way of my success.

There were no cookies in New York. I soon discovered that half of the listings in the paper were fake. I was adamant about finding an apartment on my own. No real estate agent for me—why should I pay someone close to $4,000 to find me an apartment to rent? But the agents were smart. I would see the perfect listing:

> Mid-40s apartment between 8th and 9th. Doorman building, elevator, one bedroom, lots of light! $1,600 a month.

Sounds perfect. My price range kept going up and up the more I got accustomed to the city. I started out looking to spend $1,000. By week 2, I was at $1,200; week 3, $1,300, and onward and upward. Sixteen hundred dollars sounded fine to me now. I would call the number right away.

"Hi, I am calling about the one-bedroom for $1,600 in the mid-Forties?"

"Oh, yes, I'm sorry to say that was just rented, but I have more just like it!"

That's what they all said. It was a ploy to get you to start looking with them. I still had faith I could do it myself. My dad was in real estate; it was in my blood.

The apartments that I managed to find without an agent were sad. I connected with some people from high school who were also still looking for apartments in the city. One former classmate had met a property manager who didn't run a credit check and helped young kids find their new digs. Sounded perfect. I dialed his number.

"Hello!!!" he yelled.

"Yes, is this Mr. Chang?"

"This Mr. Chang! What you want!"

Trying to sound as corporate and adult as possible: "Yes, my name is Dougall Fraser" (whenever you need to feel sophisticated, use your full name) "and I am inquiring about an apartment."

"How much you pay!"

"I am looking for an apartment between $1,600 and $1,800 a month."

"You have job?"

"Yes, I am self-employed."

"What you do!"

"I'm a life coach." Sometimes it was just easier. I didn't want to have to explain that I wasn't going to hang that neon palm in my window.

"A wha-?!"

"I'm a psychotherapist."

"A wha-?"

"I'm a *doctor*."

By the time we got off the phone, I had my Ph.D. in child psychology. *Doctor* was a word Mr. Chang understood.

"I have the apartment for rent on East Side, nice one-bedroom. I show it in an hour."

I spoke with his wife, and she gave me directions. They were both very kind. They talked about how they wanted to help young professionals find housing. How sweet. The American dream, so nicely at work here in New York. I had to cancel my next reading in order to make it to the apartment showing.

When I arrived at the building, the *entranceway* (not lobby) was similar to Beth's—maybe a tad cleaner, or more likely I was just getting used to the filth. The stairwell smelled like Adobo. I knocked on 3A.

Mr. Chang opened the door. There were about six other kids wandering the place. We were all around the same age. The living room (which had the refrigerator in it) was about 10 by 12. The kitchen had a sink and some cabinets. Above the cabinets was what looked like a large shelf.

"What is that shelf in the kitchen, Mr. Chang?"

"It's a sleeping loft," one of the other potential renters told me.

"A what?"

"You know, like if you rent this apartment, you would take the bedroom, and you can rent this bunk bed out."

Now, I want you to envision a kitchen no larger than a full-size bed, with a shelf on one wall just wide enough to hold a twin mattress. I could not stand underneath the "sleeping loft." If I were to ever dare sleep on it, I would not be able to even sit up in bed without my head hitting the ceiling. Beth's house was starting to look like a palace.

What happened to the apartment on *Friends*? Or *Seinfeld*? This was not in the brochure. Sure, people had explained to me over and over that New York apartments were smaller, but this was torture. I couldn't live like this.

I stood in the kitchen as I listened to the other kids handing in their applications. They wanted this apartment, badly. I longed to be back in Dallas, sipping a mai tai in my 1,000-square-foot loft in an historic building. What had I done? Now I had to compete with people to rent an $1,800-dollar-a-month dump that I couldn't afford anyway. I felt like a failure. Moving to New York was supposed to be a giant leap forward, but it felt like a crash and burn. (Looking back on it, I guess I wasn't able to realize that out of all the other kids, I was only one looking to rent a place on my own. The kids who got the apartment would stick one person in the living room and one on the shelf in the kitchen, and the rich one would take the bedroom.) Manhattan was a different world, a world where I needed to redefine what success looked like.

I looked at apartments on and off with Mr. Chang for months. His rents were always high, but he always had plenty of applicants. But Mr. Chang was smart—they were always rented. I finally accepted that it was going to take a lot longer to find a home than I had expected. I also needed my business to pick up so I would be able to afford any apartment that I could ever find. I needed a pick-me-up, badly. And then one night, while I was sitting in my dad's living room after a long, frustrating day, the phone rang.

"Dougall, it's Rhonda." She was a reporter for a highly-rated New York morning show. We can put you on the show tomorrow."

I was supposed to go out of town to visit my mother the next day, but I quickly cancelled my plans. Finally, this was my chance to make my mark in New York. I accepted in a hurry.

They wanted to do a man-on-the-street interview. Because of rain, we settled on a man-on-the-Long-Island-Rail-Road reading for commuters. I was nervous. Until now, all of my TV appearances had been in Texas. If I didn't like the way I came across, I just didn't send tapes of the show to anyone back home. I had complete control over what everyone in New York saw of my career. When I told my family and friends about the spot on the morning show, they were very excited. It was the first time they would get to see me live, on their own local station. It was also a major market. The viewer numbers would far surpass my TV days in Texas.

Manhattan was a different world, a world where I needed to redefine what success looked like.

Rhonda had explained to me that as we would be "in the field," they would not be doing my makeup. No makeup was simply not acceptable to me. My entire family would be watching this. My father's friends, old classmates, teachers—you name it. I wasn't about to look shiny on camera.

I decided to go to a makeup counter to get some "product." I decided on Lord & Taylor. Because my nana used to shop there, to me it will always be an old-lady store, and it seemed best for me to try not to run into anyone from my past. I walked in the ground-floor entrance of the Garden City L & T, resigned to the fact that if I was spotted, this moment would only fan the flames of gossip in our village. I could hear it already: *"I saw Dougall Fraser buying makeup!"*

I approached the MAC counter.

"Hi, I need to buy some makeup, but here's the thing. You can't touch my face or put it on me; you just need to explain it to me."

"Okay, well, what exactly is this for?" The saleswoman was puzzled.

"Well, I have to do a TV show tomorrow, and I want powder. I think?"

"Okay, sure. Let me try to figure out what shade would be good for you. . . ." She squinted at her tray, dipped a sponge in foundation, and tried to pat it on my face.

"Don't touch me!"

I was more than a little freaked out. I was not quite ready to be buying my own makeup. Why on earth I cared, I had no idea. I was not used to being in Garden City and openly gay. I spent my time there trying not to call attention to myself. Buying makeup at the local department store was not really following that rule of thumb.

The makeup artist was very kind. We negotiated on testing the product on my hand, and she explained how to apply it.

"So, you know, if you are going to a party, you just want to make sure—"

"Oh, I'm only wearing this tomorrow, one time only. For *television*," I reminded her.

"Sure."

I might as well have told her that my "friend" needed some makeup. She was not buying my story. I purchased the powder and bolted out of the store.

At 6 A.M. the next day, I jumped out of bed. I slapped on my makeup and raced out of the house. I met the producer and the field reporter at the station. Our plan was that I would do a brief interview and readings for anyone who passed by.

I did my job well, and I was treated very well. The crew was great, and the segments went very smoothly. I read for one woman who started to cry a little bit. Now, in most professions, a client crying is not exactly what you want. A hairdresser revels in her client's new look in the mirror — tears would be a disaster. For me, tears are a compliment. If someone cries, it's usually because I have struck a nerve, something very close to her heart. (Admittedly, I also knew from experience that it would mean the phone would ring with lots of new clients.)

I cannot explain how bizarre it is to mix the world of the spirits with hard, cold cash — not to mention mixing the desire to help people and do good with a desire for recognition. But when I read for someone on camera, the majority of my mind is trying to connect with him or her and bring information through my being that will uplift and inspire them. Remember the old Frosted Mini-Wheats commercial? It ran constantly in the late 1980s and early 1990s. It showed a man in a suit, sitting at his desk with a bowl of Frosted Mini-Wheats in front of him. "I like it for the fiber," he says, looking very serious and mature.

In a flash, the man becomes a little boy, dressed in the same suit, sitting at the same desk in front of the same bowl of cereal.

> I spent my time in Garden City trying not to call attention to myself. Buying makeup at the local department store was not really following that rule of thumb.

"I like it for the frosting!" the kid screams.

That is exactly what goes on in my mind when I have a great reading. As I impart wisdom to someone who actually gets tears in her eyes, the grown-up in me says:

"Maintain eye contact with her, speak clearly, and let the words flow."

While the child in me says: "Damn, I'm good!"

For me, tears are a compliment. If someone cries, it's usually because I have struck a nerve, something very close to her heart.

After the show, I went straight to my office. Both lines were ringing off the hook. If reception was not on with a live caller, they were taking messages. By the end of the day, I was booked solid for the next 6 weeks. Hello, New York! Once again, TV had done its job. I wound up doing several segments on the morning show.

THINGS WERE LOOKING UP IN NEW YORK, BUT I STILL FELT DRAWN TO CALIFORNIA. Even though I wasn't living there, I wanted to spend as much time there as possible. (To this day, my dream is to someday own a small home in northern California.) A bookstore and spiritual center called East West Bookstore in Palo Alto invited me to speak, so I decided to take the opportunity to go visit Kerry again, as the book shop was just 45 minutes south of San Francisco.

The store's events coordinator explained to me that the newsletter announcing my appearance would go out to all their customers a few weeks before I arrived on the West Coast. I had never taken a business trip before. I am a psychic—who knew from business expenses? I had no idea what to expect or how much money I would make. What if no one showed up?

I planned to stay in Palo Alto for about a week. I arrived on a Thursday night. I would do readings on Friday at the store, give a lecture that evening, do readings on Saturday, give a workshop on Sunday—then have time for possible rollover clients from the workshop over the next few days.

Palo Alto was a surprisingly expensive town. I could not find a hotel room for under $250 a night, and I was planning a 7-night stay. Finally I found the Motel 6 for $110 a night, the local no-tell motel. On this, my very first business trip, I needed to economize. I had yet to find an apartment! My office was costing much more than I had expected, and even with all my new clients, I was still having a hard time making ends meet. Also, because I was under 25, there were additional fees on my rental car. I was sure I would lose money on this trip.

When I got a good look at my room in Motel 6, it was hard to convince myself that this trip was going to be lots of fun. Using the word "functional" to describe the room would be putting it kindly. I took a hot shower and tried to prepare for my lecture that night. I called East West to check in, and the events coordinator told me they had received quite a large response.

"Dougall, your readings and workshop are sold out!"

"Really?"

"Really!" she giggled. "We have 50 people booked for your lecture tonight, but more people will show up at the door."

I was a little taken aback when I hung up the phone. It was one thing to be in Dallas and have 30 or 40 people attend a lecture in the city where I had worked and lived for so long. I had never really done any work in California—just those few days on my earlier visit, reading for friends of Kerry's. This felt bigger.

I meditated in my room for about an hour before my lecture, and as I left, I still didn't have a clue about what I would talk about. The lecture that night started at 7:30. I arrived at 6:45. Early as always.

Slowly the room began to fill. By 7:30, more than 100 people had come to hear me speak. It was the largest group I had ever appeared in front of. As they appeared, I realized that my goal for that night would be, again, to try to show people that I was not special. I'd tell them how I had learned not to take my abilities too seriously, and, more importantly, I could teach my audience how to be psychic as well. I truly believe that psychic ability is a trait that everyone possesses. I may be good at it, and it comes naturally to me, much in the way a particular sport comes easily to a professional athlete. But no matter what our abilities, we can all swing a bat and hit the ball sometimes.

I spoke that night about my journey. Stumbling my way through the world of psychic phenomena. I could feel the energy of the audience. With each sentence, they become more connected to my words, and I became more connected to them. My temperature began to rise as I continued with my talk. Now it was time to demonstrate. Normally I didn't get nervous doing readings in public, but this was a large group. I had never been paid for a lecture before, and I felt plenty of pressure. Not pressure to be right, but pressure to please. Out of 100 people, how many people should I read for? Five? Everyone?

I closed my eyes and concentrated. On the small stage, I was sandwiched between two halogen lamps, and all I could hear was their low hum. I focused on the hum and asked that the universe lead me in the right direction. Many times on TV, you will see a psychic look directly into a few hundred people, calling out random impressions they receive until an audience member confirms that they are speaking to them. This is not how I work.

Suddenly my consciousness shifted to the right. Upon opening my eyes, I gazed to the right. About five rows back, a woman's eyes caught my attention. As I looked at her, I could see her surrounded by a radiant orange hue. She would be my first reading. She was dressed like a goddess, and she had the body to match, round and feminine. At my invitation, she stood up. She was wearing a green silky pantsuit and had pulled her beautiful silver hair back in a bun. Her almond eyes squinted nervously in my direction.

"Could you please say your name for me three times?"

"Arlene, Arlene, Arlene."

"When I look at Arlene, I see a beautiful color of orange around her. This is the color of intuition. She is a healer at heart and identifies with connecting with others instantly."

Arlene nodded.

I believe psychic ability is a trait that everyone possesses. I may be good at it, much in the same way a sport comes easily to a professional athlete. But no matter what our abilities, we can all swing a bat and hit the ball sometimes.

"Arlene, I am very aware of your stomach. Have you had your gallbladder removed?"

"Yes, I have."

There was a gasp in the audience.

"As I look at you, I am so aware of my own abdomen, and something feels like it's missing. The stomach is the seat of the soul; it is our power spot. You are having health issues in this area because you do not take care of your own emotional needs. You have created an entire existence based on focusing on others. I think the universe is asking you—well, actually begging you—to become more powerful. Don't let people take advantage of you. Do you understand?"

Before I could finish those words, Arlene was crying. Not sobbing, but quietly shaking as tears came down her face. I was honored that she would share such emotion in front of a group of people.

"Arlene, do you have any questions?"

"No," she choked out.

I paused. In my eyes, Arlene looked like a queen. Dressed in silk and adorned with her orange glow, she was a beauteous, voluptuous Aphrodite.

"Arlene, I actually think you have a lot of questions. I just don't think you are used to someone asking you if you need anything."

Her eyes widened and teared even more.

I moved through the audience and did reading after reading. There was laughter and emotion in that room. It was tangible in the air. After 2½ hours, I was beat. I could feel the pull of the audience wanting more, but there was no more of me to give. I still had a full day of readings to do the following day. I closed the event to a round of applause, and with every clap, I felt my being close its channel to the other side. Afterward people crowded around me to thank me for the talk.

"That was wonderful!"

"You are so funny!"

"I have a reading with you tomorrow, and I can't wait!"

And even "Will you sign my ticket stub?"

"Are you serious?"

She was, so I signed. My first autograph.

THE EAST WEST BOOKSTORE HAS A SMALL ROOM FOR PRIVATE READINGS. I made the mistake of booking 12 appointments back-to-back the day after my lecture. I started at noon and worked straight until 6:00 with no break. Not the best idea. The room was the size of your basic walk-in closet. The far wall is painted red, and there is a tapestry hanging on the wall. There are two wicker chairs and a small table. Every time I leave the East West Bookstore, I vow that I will buy them suitable chairs for the reading room. By the end of the day, my legs are always killing me from sitting there all day. They were killing me as my last client of the day came in.

I immediately felt the pain in Pauline's heart. Her wicker chair cracked as she sat down across from me. She was too thin, wearing jeans and a T-shirt, with her hair in a no-fuss ponytail. She had the lines of a woman in middle age, yet her face had a youthful aura.

"Pauline, your heart is heavy. More heavy than people know," I started. "You had to grow up quite early. I am not sure why, but I can't see your mother. I see you, siblings, and your dad. I see you frantically running around, trying to fix everyone. This has translated into your adult life as well. You are in a failing relationship. Your husband cannot find a job, and you allow him to be lazy because you identify with taking care of the household."

"This feels like therapy," Pauline muttered.

"Well, we have to get to the heart of your emotions to understand where you are headed."

Pauline did not seem pleased with my comments. Every time I made an observation about her life, she respond with a heavy sigh.

Pauline was looking at me like I could fix anything and everything in her life. I advised her to leave her husband and focus for an entire year on just herself and her own needs. We examined the epicenter of the issue: Her mother had died when Pauline was 13, just as she was becoming a woman. Pauline had bypassed being a teenager. We spent an hour together, and Pauline was visibly moved when she left.

The feeling of being an imposter consumed me again. What kind of spiritual mentor lives at home with his dad?

By the time I arrived for my readings Sunday at the store, the events coordinator and I decided I would return in a month. By the time I left at the end of the week, the weekend of events that we'd booked for the following month was completely sold out.

On the plane ride home, I was burnt out. During the nearly 6-hour flight, I had plenty to think about. The feeling of being an imposter consumed me again. What kind of spiritual mentor lives at home with his dad? But it had been such an amazing weekend. My readings had taken a new direction. I thought about what Pauline had said when she left.

"Dougall, it has taken me 3 years in therapy to come up with what you told me in under 15 minutes."

Here I was giving such good advice. Like an adult. But when the plane landed, my dad picked me up at the airport and drove me home. In an instant, I was just a kid again.

Chapter Thirteen

PSYCHIC IN THE CITY

As many people will tell you, there is a great sense of pride and accomplishment that comes with living in New York City. I did not have this feeling.

Even though I spent 80 percent of my time in the city, my official residence was still in Garden City, living with Dad. Not only did it kill my buzz; it made dating a nightmare. I'd be out having a great time when I'd have to excuse myself for a moment at the height of the fun. . . . "Let me just call my dad and tell him I'm going to be a little late tonight." Infuriating for someone who had lived on his own since the age of 17. I must say I had become more than a little depressed over the housing situation.

I continued to go from apartment to apartment, where I was constantly turned down. Landlords would accept tenants who made half the money I made just because they had "real" jobs. "I'm sorry, but Tammye has a regular paycheck, and you do not." I carried photocopies of bank statements reflecting much higher balances than Tammye's, but my income wasn't guaranteed. I suppose I could have lived in one of Mr. Chang's places, but I am a Taurus—and our homes must be a certain way.

I finally gave in and decided it was time I contacted a real estate agent. The real estate agent and I reviewed my credit history. Not so good—that's putting it politely. It has taken me a long time to get out of debt. I remember being 18 years old and getting my first credit card in the mail. It had a $3,500 limit. Suckers! When I was 18, charging up a storm, Citibank did not explain the importance of my credit history. My friends and I would laugh and tell one another stories about the outrageous lies we told creditors when they called our houses about our overdue accounts.

"May I please speak to Dougall Fraser?"

"I'm sorry. He is out shopping," I used to answer, thinking I was very funny. I had no idea then what my flip attitude would cost me— and I do mean *cost* me—later. Back in Dallas, whenever I went to rent a house or apartment, they only looked at my renter's history. Have you been late with your rent or mortgage? Have you ever been evicted? You know—the basics. I had great letters of recommendation from every person I had rented from in Dallas. But in New York, cash and credit history talk.

I quickly figured out that to move into a Manhattan apartment of my own, I would need at least 6 months' deposit. I was looking at apartments that rented for close to $2,000 a month. That's a lot of cash to come up with. So I worked.

My New York clientele had slowly risen to the point where I was now on a par with my level of success in Dallas. And my work in California was booming. I traveled to California every other month or so. If I was at East West or just doing readings out of my hotel room, it made for a very exciting schedule. It was also going to help find me a home.

One afternoon, my real estate agent called me.

"Listen, I have an apartment on the Upper West Side. It's pretty far up, but it's a Central Park West address." I raced to the corner of Central Park West and 107th Street. It was a charming building with a doorman. It had a large lobby with a faux fireplace. It was December. A twinkly Christmas tree stood in the lobby, and garland adorned the entranceway. Nothing too fancy—it was quaint in a bed-and-breakfast kind of way. Compared with the other places I had looked at, it seemed like Trump Tower. (Which was only 40 blocks away, actually.)

The apartment was described as an "almost" one-bedroom. By that, they meant it did not have a bedroom. But for a studio, it was quite spacious. There was a separate eat-in kitchen, a large foyer, a bathroom three times the size of Beth's, and a fairly large main living area. I loved it. This time, I decided not to go the route of pretending I was a doctor. I had to meet with the board of the building. I got all dressed up and prepared a press kit of clippings boasting about my work. I was directed to an Upper East Side address to meet with Brian about the apartment.

"Dougall, so nice to meet you. How do you like the apartment?"

"Oh, it's perfect, Brian. Just perfect. I'm really looking forward to living there."

Always start with a positive. I tried to own the space by saying I was looking forward to living there—as if he had already agreed to give me the apartment.

"What do you do for a living, Dougall?"

"Well, Brian, I am a psychic."

"Really?"

"Really," I said.

> The apartment was described as an "almost" one-bedroom. By that, they meant it did not have a bedroom.

After a brief awkward moment, I said, "Just to let you know I am a very reputable psychic, I have brought with me a compilation of magazines I have been in, along with a tape of some television shows—"

"I'm sorry. I'm a little out of it today. My dog is very sick right now," Brian suddenly interrupted me.

"Oh, I'm sorry to hear that."

"You must know what I mean, Dougall."

Actually, I was not at all sure what Brian meant. It's fairly common that when I meet people and they find out I'm psychic, they think I just *know* everything about them and their current issues. Out of confusion, I just went along with him.

"I do know what you mean, Brian."

"Do dogs go to heaven?"

"I think so. In fact, it is my understanding that domesticated animals are in our lives to provide unconditional love."

Brian looked very sad. His eyes drooped, much like a basset hound's. He was a burly guy. I would expect to see him drinking Guinness and asking me about the football game, but instead we were having an Old Yeller moment. We spoke about his dog for a while, and I did my best to comfort him. By the end of the meeting, I had a new apartment.

The day I moved into the Central Park West apartment was divine. I had spent months trying to find the perfect space, and this was it. The first morning of my new commute, I felt a sense of pride. Like I really belonged in the city. No more coffee with Dad. No more Long Island Rail Road. I resumed my cushy Dallas lifestyle like there had never been an interruption.

AT THIS TIME IN THE WORLD, INTEREST IN PSYCHIC PHENOMENA WAS AT AN ALL-TIME HIGH. John Edward's show was a

bona fide hit and moved from the Sci Fi network to a major network, which was a really big deal. Psychic Sylvia Brown had about
10,000 books out. Contacting the dead was still a hot topic. I
started getting calls from everyone from major networks to random
freaks with video cameras. They all asked the same question: Do
you talk to the dead? Even if I was only
going to make a very small appearance,
they all wanted me to be John.

There was a very small news program
that I was going to be on in the tristate
area. When the segment was booked, I
made it very clear to the producer that I
was a clairvoyant, not a medium. My subjects were alive, not dead.

"Dougall, it is so nice to have you
here," the producer greeted me when I arrived. "We are going to go on the air in
about 20 minutes."

When the producer left the green-
room, I looked around at the other guests.
There was a New Age author, a young
holistic doctor, and me. We all stared at
the television monitor, watching the show
they had taped earlier that day.

The producer bustled back in.
"Dougall, you are on in about 10 minutes. Listen, we went out to the
street corner and pulled some people in. We are going to have you
contact their dead relatives, okay? Great!"

"Wait a minute! I don't talk to the dead."

"Well, haven't you ever done it?"

"Yes, but I'm not a paging system. I can't just make it happen. If

> **I do not like talking to the dead. Once I contact Aunt Tutty and we establish that she died from pancreatic cancer and had a cat named Isabella, where does that leave us?**

you tell your viewers that I talk to the dead and it doesn't happen, both you and I will look very foolish."

The producer looked annoyed. "But John Edward has such a popular show, and that's what we really want you to do."

"Then you should have contacted John Edward. I don't do that, and to be honest with you, I am not very good at it."

I do not like talking to the dead. I understand the importance of connecting with a loved one and wanting to know definitively that there is life after death. But to do that on a daily basis, quite frankly, would bore the hell out of me. Once I contact Aunt Tutty and we establish that she died from pancreatic cancer and had a cat named Isabella, where does that leave us?

I was much more interested in finding out what makes people tick. What are your strengths? What are your weaknesses? How happy a life are you living? These are my skills. I have only the highest regard for John Edward, but separating my work and myself from his approach was proving to be a much harder task than I thought.

The producer whirled around on her heels and left the room. She came back a couple of minutes later with her boss.

"Hi, Dougall, I am Lisa, the executive producer. Do we have a problem?"

Five minutes till showtime.

"Not at all. I just was telling your producer—as I had when we spoke initially—that I don't contact dead people. If you let me go out and just do readings, I promise it will be a great show."

Four minutes till showtime.

"I don't understand why you can't just do what we want!"

We were literally walking onto the set as I explained once again to Lisa it was not an exact science, nor one that I was particularly good at. I couldn't just contact anyone on command. If I could, I would probably have had breakfast with the 10th Dalai Lama.

We no longer had time to argue. I sat on the couch and was given a mike.

One minute.

I looked directly into the tele-prompter and read the words *We are here today with medium Dougall Fraser.*

As the host read those words, I watched the monitor. It showed footage of medium James Van Praagh and John Edward.

"Dougall, it is so nice to have you here."

As we moved through the interview, I totally ignored the "medium issue."

"Let's see Dougall at work!" the host said brightly.

They brought a woman on camera to join us. She sat down, and I looked directly at her.

"You have a lot of success issues. You get these from your mother. She pushed you constantly, which has led to an adult feeling of never being good enough."

"That is exactly the truth," she said.

"You will start working part-time this year, as opposed to full-time. This next year is about pleasing you, not your mom. Once you start to do that, then you will be able to conceive your own child."

"So, was Dougall accurate?" the host asked.

"That was so on target, it's scary."

> I can't just contact anyone on command. If I could, I would probably have had breakfast with the 10th Dalai Lama.

I left the studio that day with mixed emotions. I was proud that I had stuck to my guns, but I was really swimming against the tide. I wanted to do well in my career, and I couldn't ignore the thought that maybe I should become a medium. I think in any career it's natural to look up to those who are at the top of their game. It's human nature to want to be the best that we can be.

Sadly, for a while, my definition of "best" meant having my own TV show. I had fallen for the buzz. To achieve success on the level of a John Edward, I decided that I needed to be on TV every day. That's just not possible for everyone. But in Hollywood, if one network has something that works, then every network jumps on the same bandwagon. Thus began the flood of calls to my office.

> I think in any career it's natural to look up to those who are at the top of their game. It's human nature to want to be the best that we can be.

Some stood out more than others. One particular studio called me that wanted to do a show focusing on children and psychic abilities. This would not be a regular show on the air every day; it was more of a special. I was invited to come in and talk to the producer. This project seemed like a nice match for me. Because I was young, I might be easier for their target demographic to relate to. Production would take place at a haunted restaurant in the city. I would be talking to kids about ghosts and the mysteries of haunted places. I loved the idea.

When I walked into the production office, it was filled with a bunch of people exactly my age, hustling and bustling. I was brought into a room and seated in front of a small digital camera. The producer, dressed in all black with I-write-poetry facial hair, sat behind the camera.

"So, Dougall, how would you advise kids to contact a ghost?"

"Actually, I would focus more on teaching kids that in my experience as a psychic and a seer, ghosts do not really exist."

"Okay, but what if they did, and the kids wanted to contact them? How could you help them do that?"

"I guess the closest I could come to that would be to teach them how to read the energy of an area. Like psychometry. Psychometry is the ability to take an object and tune in to its former owner or what energy is connected to it."

"Would you use a Ouija board?"

"No, I don't think they work."

"What kind of things would you need for this séance?"

"Well, it's not really a séance. I would teach the kids to follow their own hearts. They don't need tricks or tools to see energy."

"Would you use black candles?"

The interview was much shorter than I had expected, though I'm sure it took much longer than they wanted. I was certainly not the psychic they were looking for. They wanted a gypsy or a "ghostbuster." Perhaps if I informed him that lamb's blood would be needed, I would have gotten the job.

There were others, like the interesting gentleman who wanted to do a psychic version of *The McLaughlin Group*. But the majority of the calls were people looking for mediums. That was just not me.

I finally decided that I was going to try to ignore the television world and focus more on just being good at what I did every day. My new goal was to redefine what success meant to me. It was not going to be determined in how much airtime I got. Or the size of my paycheck, or whether or not ABC would allow me to sit next to Regis every day. My priority was to stay true to my clients, my abilities, and my original goal—to help people live up to their highest potential.

I added a statement to my Web site that was fairly basic but went straight to the heart of what I was trying to do. I stated that my goal in my work was to help people connect with their purpose. Why are you here on this planet, and what can you do to make your life the best it can be? But, as often happens in my work, my clients were mirroring to me the same issues I was struggling with. We were all wondering how to define success on our own terms. But even once I'd come to some clarity myself, I was still finding that it didn't matter what I said to some of my clients about purpose and satisfaction—if they weren't going to be rich and famous, they were extremely disappointed.

> **But, as often happens in my work, my clients were mirroring to me the same issues I was struggling with. We were all wondering how to define success on our own terms.**

"Do you see anything about my screenplay?" a new client asked anxiously. Rob was a straight man, early thirties, whose girlfriend had bought the appointment for him—my least favorite situation because, let's be honest, Rob would not be sitting in my office were it not for his girlfriend.

"Let's see. I can see why you would enjoy writing one. You have a captivating way of seeing the world. I think that's why your friends enjoy your company so much. You're funny. I would work on short films."

"But I'm writing a blockbuster action movie," Rob mumbled.

"Well, you are not making money from your writing right now, correct?"

"Correct."

"Have you ever thought about being a teacher?"

"I *am* a teacher."

"Great! I think that is a large part of your destiny. The creative work—screenwriting—seems more of a personal thing. You enjoy it; it helps you define yourself. But I just don't see it creating a living for you."

"But I want it to."

"By all means, I would continue to try and write more scripts and produce and stay as much in the creative venues as you can. But you have asked me for my prediction, and my prediction is that you will continue to teach. In teaching, I see a very rewarding life for you."

Rob crossed his arms and his body structure became rigid. He was no longer making eye contact with me. He was mad. Mad at me.

"I'm sorry, Rob. I wish I could say something else, but I won't lie to you. You should test me. Nothing would please me more than for you to win an Oscar and come back here to say, 'Dougall Fraser, you were dead wrong.' But for a minute, let's talk about why you are so obsessed with this idea. If you could do anything for a living, what would it be?"

"I would be a big-time Hollywood mogul, like Steven Spielberg."

"So you really love to write?"

"I do."

"Well, then, continue to write. I invite you, though, not to worry about becoming the next Steven Spielberg. Be Rob. Write not to get your name in lights but because you can't think of anything other than writing."

"This sucks!"

I could not blame Rob for being frustrated. It sometimes seemed that everybody I saw wanted to be famous. I was reading for a lot of struggling writers and actors, plus everyone else. Everyone—from a housewife and mother of six to the CEO of a big corporation to a gardener—they all told me some variation of "I can actually sing." Or "All my friends say I could be a model." How can I say this tactfully? If you're really model material, they take a Polaroid of you and send you to Milan. When you're 14, not when you're 35.

> **It sometimes seemed that everybody I saw wanted to be famous. Everyone— from a housewife and mother of six to the CEO of a big corporation—all told me some variation of "I can actually sing."**

I have a great friend who I believe is really talented. Do I think she'll ever be starring on Broadway? No. Is she gifted and funny, and will she do her own one-woman show in a 16-seat room off-off-Broadway, not a theater? Absolutely. And I honor her more because for her, it's more about working and perfecting her craft than exploiting some effortless natural ability.

I always tell actors, "You need to decide why you're doing this. Will you be happy with dinner theater in Cedar Rapids, or are you doing this to get your name up in lights?" I am always amazed at how pissed off people get when I tell them they are not going to reach the A level of fame. Now, mind you, that's not even a psychic thing— that's simple math. Statistically, out of all the struggling actors and models and writers in our country, fewer than 2 percent of them make a living from their craft. I can count on one hand the times when I've read for someone I thought was really going to make it—and they were already well on their way by the time they came to see me.

I tried to blend in some life coaching along with my (often disappointing) prediction for their level of professional success in the arts.

"So, when's the last time you went on an audition?"

"Well, it's been a while. . . . I get really nervous and . . ." Yeah, right. You want to be the star of a Paramount movie, and the biggest thing you've done was play Annie in your junior high school play. That's not going to cut it. But the people who are out there hustling and auditioning and it's an integral part of their life? I respect and admire them, no matter what "success" they may achieve.

I think we live in an age that defines "success" the wrong way. Every other client who comes to me wants to be a reality television star. They want to be wealthy and have their house on *MTV Cribs*. People equate success with money. When we have these grandiose ideas of what happiness looks like, it can lead to misery. I had certainly been struggling with this conflict myself! But it was right about this stage when I began to discover that success lies in contentment.

Every day, I see countless people who walk around New York in misery because they're not famous and they don't have a movie deal and they haven't found the love of their life and they don't have a six-bedroom mansion in the Hamptons. But then you see the librarian who makes $16,000 a year and loves her job and is very, very happy. I was no different—I was wrestling with the idea that lots of money and a television show would be the only way I could define success. I had yet to come to my ultimate understanding with myself: that I would rather do one reading a day that was true to who I am than waste my time and the client's trying to make everybody feel good.

When I tell someone like Rob that he is not going to write a screenplay that grosses more than $20 million, he is usually disappointed and pissed off. But it's not as if I'm telling him that he can't write! In fact, I bet he is quite a talented writer, but maybe his stuff is too edgy, not mainstream. I have read for plenty of people like Rob. So many that sometimes I despair at ever getting them to take from my reading what I wanted them to, which was to recognize the miracles of life. Perhaps I was even more frustrated with the Robs in my practice during this period in my life because I was not seeing my own miracles.

I had come so far in my career. And I had started from scratch a number of times. But was I really appreciating my own success? As soon as I moved into Manhattan, I got caught up in that cycle of comparisons that can eat away at your soul. I could not help but feel as though I was "less than" for not living in a one-bedroom place. I was ashamed that my neighborhood was considered to be in *transition*. Five years ago, it was probably not the best area to walk around in the middle of the night. Two years ago, you still had to be careful. It's not like there were needles on the street and constant muggings, but it was certainly a neighborhood going through changes. I used to get myriad reactions to my address.

"Where do you live?" someone would ask casually.

"I live on Central Park West and 107th Street."

"Ohhh . . . fancy!"

Same party, different person: "Where do you live?"

"I live on Central Park West and 107th."

"My God, is that safe?"

Depending on the situation I was in, I would answer that question accordingly. If I was at a function where I felt insecure—a business event, for example—I usually responded with "I live on Central Park West." Well, Central Park West stretches for about 110 blocks. I might as well just have said I live "around."

Rather than owning who I was, I was standing in the way of my own miracle. I could have told people the story of how I had moved and struggled and was finding my way. But I was ignoring all of that. I was helping other people see it, but I couldn't see it myself. To get to my own point of clarity, I needed to own my circumstance.

I continued to see little parts of myself in each person that came to see me. It was kind of bizarre. For so many years, I had tried my hardest to remove myself from the reading itself. These people were coming to me for advice. I had always felt as though I needed to be the more evolved person, when in essence, I was just like my clients. Some days I still wanted to be rich and famous with my own TV show! I wondered if I would ever find true love. I still struggled with money. How to reconcile these feelings with my message, which I truly believed?

I started to examine everything I did. Every word that I said suddenly became more weighted and important. My focus turned from pleasing people to being authentic. And I had opportunities to be authentic on every level, for every kind of person. Rob the writer was just an example; my days were filled with a profusion of lifestyles and situations.

> **I was helping other people see it, but I couldn't see it myself. To get to my own point of clarity, I needed to own my circumstance.**

I am somewhat of a voyeur—it's partially why I love my job. My days are filled with people from all walks of life. I might start my day with someone like Steven, a thin young gay man, quite a successful drag queen in New York City. He made the appointment to focus on his love life. Next I might see an attorney—a well-dressed, corporate heterosexual man, but with the exact same concerns as Steven.

With both clients, I talk about the lessons of love. Such different lifestyles and yet the same lessons. I think they would both be surprised to know I had told each of them the same thing, which boils down to: If you want to fall in love, then you need to date. Both of them spent too much time at the office, though for the attorney that meant poring over depositions until the wee hours of the night, and for Star-Letta it was lip-synching "Gypsies, Tramps, and Thieves" until dawn. But in the end, I gave them both the same homework: *In the next month, I want you to initiate two dates. Stop living your life through your career; if you want to be in love, then you have to work at it.*

My clients continued to fascinate me. Apart from money and fame, they were all looking for the same thing. Everyone is looking for the same answers. *Why am I here? Will I be loved?* Love did not mean just in the romantic sense. Love can manifest in the form of fans of your "blockbuster" movie or a raise at your job or a brand-new friendship. But what people tend to mean when they ask about romantic love is "Will I find my soul mate?"

I could write an entire book on soul mates. I spend most of my days making predictions about love and, even more often, listening to people's confusion about relationships.

"There is a relationship that you just got out of that seems to be creating total confusion for you."

Katie was a new client. She had actually flown in for the session. That's rare, but it has been known to happen. She was sophisticated, wrapped in a pashmina, very attractive. Obviously she had plenty of money. I couldn't help but stare at her flawless skin. Her eyes were wide and slightly reddened from tears. We had just begun, but I didn't have to be psychic to know that she was filled with sadness.

Apart from money and fame, everyone is looking for the same answers.

Why am I here?

Will I be loved?

"I did just get out of a relationship," she choked out.

"It's so bizarre because I don't see a breakup. It just feels like it's over. Does that makes sense?"

"Yes."

In my mind, I saw a heart with an X over it. My soul filled with disappointment. He seemed to be the perfect match for her.

"Katie, this man was special, at first. I can see why you were so interested in him. He is remarkable. Or should I say *was* remarkable."

"I know. Why aren't we together?"

"Katie, in life there is more work than we are told about. When you meet an individual and you share a special relationship, it is an amazing cosmic occurrence. But after that, the duration of how long you stay together is up to you."

Katie told me that she had been engaged for 6 months to a man she adored. Every month that brought them closer to the date, his personality changed for the worse, until he became someone she barely recognized. Her fiancé was from a broken home. He had never met his father, and he was totally petrified of relationships.

"Based on what I see and what you have told me, I do not think that he can give you the kind of relationship that you want. The choice in leaving him was wise. Mark my words: He will try and get back together with you. But you need to try and figure out what kind of relationship you want. There is potential to connect with another man out there, one who has the capacity to recognize who you are. Your last fiancé was unable to do that."

Katie and I talked for a long time about philosophies of love. She had the same misconception that many of the people I speak to have. She wanted someone to complete her—and outside of Tom Cruise movies, this is not possible.

> **She wanted someone to complete her—and outside of Tom Cruise movies, this is not possible.**

"Katie, I want to give you some homework. I want you to go home and write down a spiritual personal ad. Describe yourself. And then focus on the kind of relationship you want. How much time do you spend together? Is he fearless? Is he passionate? When you finish the ad, read through it. If your fiancé is like the person you have just fantasized about, then go back to him. If he is remarkably different, there is your answer."

Two weeks later, I got a letter from Katie. She had followed my advice and was moving forward. During her session, I had been right to advise her not to look for an individual to complete her. As usual, I hadn't planned on it, but the words had just flowed from my mouth. But God forbid I should listen to myself.

After a bumpy year, my career in New York was going very well. I was finally learning a few of my own lessons. I wasn't rich or famous or a best-selling author, but I was happy. At least in my work. Dating was a bit of a nightmare. I have never been very good at it. I was more of a relationship kind of guy, which is kind of funny, considering I had not been in many. I had a circle of friends, each of whom seemed to always have a boyfriend. New guys or girls on a constant basis. How was it that I could help people attune themselves to love, but all the men I met were so far from what I really wanted?

Chapter Fourteen

LOOKING FOR LOVE
IN ALL THE WRONG PLACES

I HAD ALWAYS BEEN SURE THAT I WOULD FIND THE LOVE OF MY LIFE INSTANTLY ONCE I MOVED TO NEW YORK. I would sit at a café, sipping tea, making eye contact with men as they passed, just waiting for someone to approach me.

That was the problem—waiting for someone to approach me. I could stand in front of a group of hundreds and give a lecture for over an hour with nothing prepared, and though I would be a little nervous, it always went fine. But sitting in a café and striking up a conversation with someone I was attracted to? Not going to happen.

In the fall of 2003, I decided it was time I focused on stepping out of my comfort zone with love. That is an expression I use with clients so often, I could have it continually spooling on an audiotape during my sessions. Because I work for myself, meeting people in the office was impossible. And just like in Dallas, my home had once again become my office. I decided to work out of my apartment so I could save money in the hopes of someday buying an apartment. So from time to time, just to get out into the energy of the world, I would take my laptop to a café and work on some writing. One of my favorite locations was Le Gamin, a French-style café in the heart of Chelsea. In the midafternoon, it's quiet and a good place to work, read, or sometimes see cute boys.

One Wednesday afternoon, I decided to put on the I-always-meet-a-man sweater and venture out. (Don't laugh—this sweater had magic powers.) I sat down at Le Gamin, ordered a cup of mint tea, and opened the computer. As happened on most days I planned to write, I just sat there and stared at the screen. After gazing at my lighted box for an hour or so with no inspiration in sight, I glanced over to my right and noticed another gentleman sitting alone. He was cute, in a bookish sort of way. He looked right at me and smiled. I quickly looked away. My heart was pounding. I picked up my tea and took a sip, trying to appear ever so calm even though the china was practically clinking in my hand. *Okay, Dougall, you can do this—just say hi!*

Mind you, if I had been in Barracuda—another Chelsea location—I would have had no problem saying hello to this stranger, as I would have been holding an adult tea, as opposed to herbal. But here my defenses were up; I did not have any liquid courage. I looked over at Bookish Boy, and he smiled again. I smiled back and started to type. After about 15 minutes, he got up and left.

I waited for over an hour with fantasies dancing in my head. Any minute now, the waitress would come over and deliver a note that said, "You are adorable—here is my number." She passed by a few times, but delivered nothing. I fantasized that he would return to the café, stride over to my table, sit down across from me, push the screen of my laptop away, and begin to talk. That didn't happen either.

Finally I left—alone. This was typical. I was not stepping out of my comfort zone at all. That night I met a friend for dinner.

"I need a date," Beth said.

"I do, too."

I told Beth about my Bookish Boy and how I never said anything to him. As I relayed the story, I realized that it wasn't really about Bookish Boy. It was about my lack of drive. By the end of our bottle of wine, we both resolved to *really* step out of our comfort zones. Both of us vowed to initiate conversations with men.

"Have you ever asked a guy out, Beth?"

"I never have. It's different for straight girls."

"That is so not true! I think it's the same."

As we walked out of the restaurant, we turned to face Gramercy Park. A dark, handsome man walked by. He was about 6'1", jet black hair, well-dressed.

"Gay or straight?" I asked.

"He's so *gay*—go talk to him!"

"Excuse me, sir," I said, emboldened.

He turned around, looking a little alarmed. "Yes?"

"Do you know anywhere fun around here to go for a drink?"

I did not want him to think I was a tourist, so I added, "I live on the West Side."

"Um . . . let me see."

He looked at Beth, not a good sign for me, but possibly for her.

"I don't think there are any gay bars around here. . . ." I was fishing.

"Well, I wouldn't really know."

Dammit. Straight. A few minutes of conversation confirmed it. He and Beth began to talk. He joined us for a drink right then, and they set a time to meet the following week. It figured that the one time I stepped out of my comfort zone, I found someone who was not an option. Maybe it was subconscious. Maybe I wasn't really ready to do it for myself. One thing I did know: I was ready to try something.

I was far from alone in my problem. There is a fairly common scene with my clients that I see with love, over and over, every day. And that is lack of effort.

"What do you see for my love life?" Dan leaned forward as he asked this question. Dan was a gay man in his midthirties. He worked for a major magazine. Attractive—intimidatingly attractive. He was wearing jeans and a T-shirt, but the shirt was glued perfectly to every part of his body. He had blondish hair—a dye job, I'm sure—but the Ryan Seacrest look worked for him.

Did you ever just see someone and want to freeze time? I just wanted to stare for about a minute or ask, "Do you know how good-looking you are?"

Instead, I said, "Well, at the moment I see a lack of a love life."

"Very true," he laughed.

"Actually, you don't seem to make much effort with love. When is the last time you had a date?"

"What do you mean by a date?"

"Well, I mean dinner, a movie, drinks, the museum—whatever—something before a sexual encounter."

"It's been about a year."

"Well, Dan, it's up to you. Don't get me wrong. I realize that sex is an important part of life, but what about incorporating an exchange that is not just based on carnal passion?"

"What do you mean?"

"Okay, first let me make some predictions about love. There is a man that you will meet who is fairly tall—about 6'2". He has sandy-colored hair and light eyes. I see a big letter T in my head. I know this seems odd, but I also see Flo Jo, the Olympic athlete. I don't know what that means, but that's what I see."

"How can he be black and have sandy-colored hair?"

"Good question, Dan! Anyway, now here is your homework. My understanding of soul mates is that timing is up to you. I think it is your destiny to meet the man we will call Mr. T. *When* you meet him is up to you. At the rate you are going, you are not making any effort to connect with men. I'm not telling you to stop having sex, but what I am suggesting to you is getting to know someone when you sleep with them."

"I do! It's just I never get asked out."

"Well, what about becoming more proactive with dating. Your homework in the next month is to go on three separate dates that you initiate."

"Homework?"

"Remember, Dan, the universe works as hard as you do. It's a give-and-take relationship. I am not saying that if you ask out three men, one of those men will be Mr. Right, but I am saying that it will get the energy in motion. By using the law of attraction, you are stating to the universe that you are ready for the One."

After the session, I realized how often I was giving this advice. The faces changed, but the message was the same. It might be a young person just getting out of college who had no dating experience at all. Or a newly divorced man now in his late fifties who had completely forgotten about the art of courting a woman. Different people, same confusions and desires. I would make predictions and then blend in some advice as well, and the approach

> My understanding of soul mates is that timing is up to you. It is your destiny to meet someone, but *when* you meet him or her is up to you.

seemed to be working. Slowly but surely, letters and e-mails started to come in about the great results clients had gotten from taking my advice.

Dan, in fact, came back to see me in person about 6 months later.

"I did what you said."

"I'm sorry, Dan. I don't quite remember our conversation."

This is always an awkward moment. In the 6 months since Dan had seen me, I am sure I had done several hundred other readings. I had spoken to people from all over the world. It's not for lack of interest that I couldn't recall Dan; it's from lack of memory space.

"Well, I came in here, and I thought you were crazy. You told me that I was not making enough effort with love and needed to make connections with people. When I left your office, I felt really annoyed. I had been going out and meeting guys and even having sex. So I didn't really notice that I was lonely. My therapist and I talked about what you said, and she agreed wholeheartedly. So I tried. I asked a few guys out. I even put out a personal ad! And then it happened."

Dan reminded me of his prediction: Mr. T, sandy-colored hair, and Flo Jo. He was at the gym when he made eye contact with a man running on the treadmill. He walked right up to the guy and struck up a conversation. Lo and behold, his name was Tom, and he was training for the marathon.

"We dated for about 3 months, and it was superb. The guy was great."

I had been right about the characteristics and even the first letter of this man's name. But sadly the relationship hadn't worked out. Why? To be honest, I have no idea.

"I realize that you said we would be together for a while, Dougall, and that was wrong. But I'm not mad. You really showed me a good lesson about life—that what I give, I get back."

I have always said that I really think I can only be about 80 percent accurate. And I am sure there are skeptics out there that will read this story and say, "Look—you were wrong." I do understand their perspective. How many men whose names start with the letter T are in your gym right now? Chances are, a few. And statistically, gay men do tend to work out. To say that I see a famous runner could manifest in a number of ways, not necessarily in training for a running competition. But that's not how I understand it. I truly believe that I was perceiving a blockage in Dan's energy, and my predicting this relationship helped give him the power to take command of his love life.

But despite helping others make their moves toward love, I still hadn't made any big moves in my own life. As a kid, when I meditated, I used to sit in silence and see a man in the distance of my vision. He had dark hair and eyes, and I could not really make out his appearance. There was one thing I knew for sure: He was Jewish. I have always had a thing for Jewish men, but none were forthcoming. Where was *my* Jewish husband?

As if to underscore my loneliness, all the single people I knew were falling in love right and left. Every time I turned around, I was going to another wedding. It felt like everyone was either engaged or getting married. I, on the other hand, was more single than ever.

I became newly committed to taking my own advice and becoming more proactive with dating. I decided to put out a personal ad, which was a lot harder than I thought. How exactly was I to describe what I was looking for in 30 words or less? Not to mention that the personals had an entire foreign language—SGWM, ISO, BiCurious? I had a lot to learn.

I joined a service on the Internet where I had to fill out a questionnaire describing myself and what qualities I was looking for. One of the questions was about my occupation. A perfectly reasonable question. I was honest; I listed my occupation as psychic. I sent my personal ad out into cyberspace and awaited my prince.

Days went by without a single response. I decided I needed to be more proactive and respond to other people's ads. Still I heard nothing. My only guess was that it had to be my job scaring people off. I could only imagine what people envisioned when they thought about contacting a potential psychic mate. I decided to remove "psychic" from the occupation question. Instead of listing my job, I simply stated: "My job tends to scare people away." That would keep them guessing!

Instead of listing my job, I simply stated: "My job tends to scare people away." That would keep them guessing!

Within an hour, I had three responses.

Most of the men that responded to me were much older—in their fifties. I was not quite sure what part of "ISO of GM age 24–34" was not clear. But I was inundated with men in their fifties who assured me that they were "young at heart." That's all well and good, but it was too much of an age difference for me. I'm not Celine Dion.

The few that I talked to seemed relatively sane. I went out with a couple of them, and they were perfectly nice men, but there was just no connection.

It was a Saturday night, and I had to go to another engagement party, this time for some friends on Long Island. I rode with Beth and her boyfriend, Lenny. Beth was now happily in love. She had seen Lenny in a bar and initiated a conversation. (Her move out of the comfort zone worked—they are now married.) On our way home, I was antsy. I was just itching to meet someone.

Beth and Lenny dropped me off at my apartment. I took my suit off in the living room and put on a pair of shorts and a T-shirt. I replayed the entire night in my head. I was lonely. There was a part of me that felt sad that I was attending another celebration for people who were about to spend the rest of their lives together, while I was still coming home to an empty apartment. Out of sheer loneliness, I decided to log on to the Internet. I hadn't been in a chat room in quite some time.

Even as I write these words, I am mortified to admit that this is true. It was about 2 A.M., and I was in New York City. I received an instant message from a guy that lived in my neighborhood, or at least close enough. His name was David. For fear that it could possibly be a client, I told him my name was Sean. We talked for a minute via the Internet—we both said that we were up and bored.

I gave him my telephone number. I can tell a lot from someone's voice—it's how I do my work, after all. When I answered the phone, from the moment I first heard David's voice, I felt very comfortable. We talked for about 20 minutes. I told him about my night; he told me about his. And finally I asked if he wanted to come over. David lived about 20 blocks from my apartment, exactly a mile. Not too far. I can't believe that I invited him over. This was not the kind of behavior a professional psychic and life coach should be engaging in. What would my clients think? What would my mother think? What would the doorman think? The hell with that—what was I thinking? I know what I was thinking. I was lonely, and I was looking for a warm body. I had no idea what it would turn into.

When I opened the door, I was greeted by a handsome man. David is 6', with short, dark hair and the kindest eyes I have ever seen.

His head was tilted to the side as he gave me a shy smile. As we made eye contact, these words passed through my mind: *I love you.* I told myself that I must be drunk. But I wasn't drunk; I had been home for over an hour and hadn't really had that much to drink at the party. But something in my being responded strongly and immediately to the man standing in the hall. I invited this stranger in.

We sat down on my couch and started to talk.

"I like your apartment, Sean."

Oh, dear, I had told him my name was Sean. Perhaps I should tell him now that wasn't my real name. But it would sound so strange—what kind of a person lies about their name in the middle of the night? What kind of person *invites* a stranger over in the middle of the night? I should have grown out of this stage. I was 25 years old and a spiritual mentor. But I had lied about my name, and I had invited him over, and he was here. And he was really sweet.

"Actually, my name is Dougall."

I made up some kind of excuse about why I had lied about my name. We spent what was left of the night talking. I knew in my heart that he would be a very important part of my life, but my mind told me that I was crazy.

The following day, I was shocked to see that he had called. In my experience,

This was not the kind of behavior a psychic and life coach should be engaging in. What would my clients think? What would my mother think? What would the doorman think? The hell with that—what was I thinking?

that didn't really happen. I saved that first message he left for a long time. He asked me to join him for dinner. He did not say "grab a bite" or "do you want to go out" or "let's get together this weekend." It was a Sunday night, and he wanted me to join him for dinner. I said yes.

David was the first man I had been out with who didn't ask me lots of questions about work and my career. On most dates, I have found that you can fill a lot of time talking about each other's profession. At the time, David had just been laid off from a job in computers that he had despised. Another good sign. What I noticed the most was that he seemed to just accept what I did without any explanation. He was interested, but not too interested. This was truly refreshing.

That week I had lunch with my good friend Meredith at the Moonstruck Diner on the corner of Twenty-third and Ninth. I could go to any diner in America and be very happy. No matter what time of day it is, a cup of coffee at a diner is perfection.

"I met the man that I am going to marry," I announced.

"Oh, really?" Meredith's eyes were sparkling.

Meredith was a massage therapist in the chiropractor's office where I worked when I first moved to the city. I can't be around her for more than 10 minutes without my stomach hurting from laughter.

I explained to her the story of meeting David and the proper date we had the following night.

"You're such a slut!" she exclaimed.

"Stop! I can't explain it, but something is different about him. I can feel it."

"Well, don't tell him that you think you will marry him. That's sure to scare him away!"

She was right. But I was not really afraid of scaring him away. I was afraid of being wrong. Here I was, psychic Dougall Fraser, and what if I told everyone what an amazing experience I had with this guy and I was wrong?

That week, David and I made plans for one more date. He was leaving for Florida to go take a real estate exam back in Miami, where he grew up. Friday night was our third date—second official.

For years, I'd had requirements as to what I wanted in a man. There were three things that I thought were critical. I wanted someone who had gone to therapy. I wanted someone who was totally out. And they had to have a career.

As David and I sat at the restaurant, eating dinner, I asked him, "Are you out to your family?"

This was crucial for me. I worked for many years to be proud of myself as a gay man, and I was in search of someone who was also proud of his life.

For David, the circumstances were different. He had come out to his parents just about a year before. He had not received the best reaction. David's parents have an amazing story. They moved from Israel with very little in their pockets, and through hard work and the American dream, they built an amazing life for themselves. They are still very connected to the ways of their culture—but that culture does not have much to say about gay and lesbian people.

As David spoke, my heart went out to him. I could see the pain in his eyes. The fear of not being accepted. He was very candid. He told me the entire story, and in that moment one of my requirements for love flew out the window. I no longer cared that he was not out to everyone in his life. He was so courageous. I can't imagine how I would have handled it if my family had reacted differently.

When the bill arrived, we bickered over who would pay. He won.

We walked out of the restaurant.

"Look—Isabella Rossellini!" David pointed across the street.

Most of the time, I am all for a celebrity sighting. This time, I barely even glanced over. I could not take my eyes off him.

The following morning, David left to spend 3 weeks in Florida. There was a definite possibility he would move back in with his parents and start working in real estate. If he passed the test, he would move. I have never wanted someone to fail a test more in my life.

For those 3 weeks, we spoke every single night. We talked about families and coming-out issues. We talked about my work and my struggles to create a practice I could be proud of. What I realized was that David had the most amazing ability to communicate, better than anyone I had ever met. And he made me feel wonderful.

Having him gone for 3 weeks seemed like torture, but it also helped. Our time spent together was not over dinner or at a movie or all of the typical things that you do when you are first dating. All we had were our voices and conversation.

It's funny to me how my requirements for love seemed so important at the time. David may not have been out to his entire world, and he may have been searching for a career, but what is most important is that he could communicate. He had aspirations to become a makeup artist. He was preparing to come out to his sisters. He was a good man. He was also pretty darn cute.

Chapter Fifteen

───◆───

AMERICA'S MOST WANTED . . . PSYCHIC

DAVID MADE THE DECISION TO RETURN FROM FLORIDA, LIVE IN NEW YORK, AND SEEK A NEW CAREER. After a few weeks of togetherness, I was completely sold. I was sure he was the guy for me. We spent the spring and summer attached at the hip, and every day was wonderful.

The more time we spent together and the closer we became, the more curious David became about my work. Most people want to see a demonstration of my psychic abilities, which I totally understand. I think it's fair to say that the proof is in the pudding. But at this point in my life, the psychic part of my life has become almost a separate entity.

Though I consider myself to be a very spiritual person, the only time that my psychic ability really manifests itself is when I am at work. That is not to say that I don't perceive things or know things on my own, just like everybody else. The truth is that predicting my own future doesn't really interest me. After all the time and effort, the years spent becoming a very good psychic, I prefer to live my own life in the now. So I have a pretty strict rule: I don't read for family or friends, and that includes David.

> After all the time and effort, the years spent becoming a very good psychic, I prefer to live my own life in the now.

"So when are you going to give me a reading?" David asked.

We were sitting on his couch. Love seat is actually the proper term. I am 6'6" and David is 6'—cuddling on a love seat is partly a form of limb-twisting torture.

"I can't read for you. I care about you too much."

"I don't understand that."

"Well, the only thing I can tell you is it would be too hard for me to separate what I want for you from what actually is predestined for you. For example, I of course would like to 'see' that we are going to be together for the next 50 years. But because my own desires and emotions are involved, it makes it harder for me to actually know what will happen."

"But sometimes I feel like you know those things and you don't tell me. Or it feels like you can read my mind."

I cannot read minds, nor would I want to, though I have grown accustomed to hearing this repeatedly from people I am close to over the years. But somehow, hearing these words from the man that I was falling in love with made me sad. Was he afraid of me?

I tried to respond as honestly as I could. "The only thing I can tell you, David, is that I will be able to perceive feelings in you that some people may overlook. You may have a smile on your face, but I will know that something is actually quite wrong. I won't know what that something is, and I won't be able to fix it for you. I will be able empathize with you, perhaps on a deeper level than a lot of people. That can be a nice feeling."

After reassuring David that I could not read his mind, he seemed a little more relaxed. And from what I later learned, it was all for the best that I was unable to divine his every thought. You see, my friend Janna and I have a similar obsession that is not exactly the healthiest one. You name any diet, and we are ready to try it. I have not had to be on any kind of a diet for about 6 or 7 years, but still to this day, I just can't ignore the newest diet trend. Optifast, Slim-Fast, low-fat, cabbage soup, Weight Watchers, South Beach, no carb, vegetarian, vegan . . . at some point I have tried them all. Right around the time David and I were falling in love, Janna got me on Atkins.

"I've decided to try the Atkins diet for a full month," Janna announced.

We were on the phone, where much of our relationship takes place. Janna and I are both self-employed, so phone calls during the day are our version of water cooler breaks in a regular office.

"It's great! I have a friend who has lost so much weight, and there are so many fun foods you can still eat. Cheese, any dairy, really. Meat, chicken . . ."

She listed the foods that you could enjoy with such enthusiasm that by the time she was finishing her sentence, I was an immediate Atkins convert.

"I just started it 2 minutes ago!" I said.

For the next 3 weeks, I was the poster child for the carnivore revolution. Eggs and dairy were regular staples at every meal. No more skim milk in my coffee—I was a real man, a half-and-half kind of a guy.

During this phase, Janna and I met for dinner each night, alternating houses. We would almost try to top each other with the tastiest and most Atkins-friendly meal that could possibly be prepared.

"Tonight I am serving T-bone steak with blue cheese dressing." Janna seemed so proud as she placed the carcass on the table.

"Tonight we are having pepper-steak-with-bacon hors d'oeuvres!" I'd say the next night at my apartment. Clearly, I showed her.

It was sickening. My body felt like a frying bin at a McDonald's. And, of course, as with any diet, whatever food I am not allowed to eat is what I crave the most. I dreamed of pasta and bread. Glasses of wine over potatoes au gratin. I missed my carbs, and I missed them bad.

"You have got to check your pH balance." Janna had the look of a mad scientist in her eye one night.

"My what?"

"Ketosis! It's the first phase of the diet. Your pH balance! Here— take this piece of litmus paper and go pee."

"Are you crazy? What the hell is ketosis?"

"I did it. It's not working for me. My pH balance is all fucked-up. I'm sure I am gaining weight even as we speak." Bacon was frying in the background as I closed the door to the bathroom.

I think it's pretty safe to say that you have serious food issues when you are in the bathroom, peeing on a stick of paper to see if you're in ketosis. As I looked down at the strip of paper, it instantly became a bright pink.

"Janna, I'm pregnant!"

With great pride, I showed her my ketosis results. According to Dr. Atkins, I was burning fat like a freight train! Little did I know that Dr. Atkins practically cost me the greatest love of all.

A few months later, David and I traveled to San Francisco, partly for my work and partly to take our first trip together. We were sitting on the patio of one of my favorite restaurants in the Castro, Namaste Indian Cuisine.

I took my last bite of Asian noodle.

"You know, I was trying to find any excuse not to like you in the beginning," David told me.

"Really, like what?"

"Do you remember when we were first together, you were on the Atkins diet?"

"Oh, yeah." It seemed so long ago. By this time, I had given up the Atkins diet. I was currently obsessed with my favorite diet—the work-out-five-times-a-week-and-eat-whatever-I-want diet.

"Well, it used to give you terrible breath." He giggled.

"What! Are you serious? Why didn't you say anything?"

I was mortified. It is true—a no-carb, ketosis-lovin' fool will have rank breath. I thought I'd been so careful—I used to pop Altoids like Rush Limbaugh with a bottle of OxyContin.

"At first I thought I was making it up. But then I noticed that when you stopped the diet, it instantly went away, and you've been minty fresh ever since—well, most of the time." He giggled again.

"I told you I couldn't read your mind! Don't you think if I could, I would have mainlined an IV of Scope directly into my body?"

He realized what I was saying. This was proof positive I could not tell what he was thinking. I could not sneak into the private confines of his mind to search for answers. When we were together, we were equals.

But he was still curious about seeing me in psychic action. We had decided that the best place for him to see me work would be in some kind of public format. Maybe television or a speaking engagement. I waited for the perfect opportunity.

IN THE FALL OF 2003, I GOT A CALL from *The John Walsh Show* on NBC. John Walsh is mostly known for his courageous efforts on the nationally admired *America's Most Wanted*. He also, for about 3 years, hosted his own daytime talk show. When I received the initial call, I was a little surprised, figuring that any programming with his name attached to it would be geared toward crime fighting and or missing persons. Both are areas that I tend to stay away from. There are numerous psychics out there that claim to have the ability to solve major crimes. Again, not my strong suit. I'd like to think of myself more as the Marianne Williamson or the Suze Ormond of the psychic world, rather than a psychic detective.

When I returned the call, I was told I was being considered for a show called *Dream Jobs*. The concept being that I was someone with a remarkable talent and an unusual career. The original plan was for me to appear during a segment and talk about my work, and hopefully bring a client with me to discuss how I had changed his or her life.

"Dougall, would you mind coming down to the studio so everyone can meet you?"

Of course I agreed, though I must admit that the paranoid part of my mind was absolutely positive that *The John Walsh Show* wanted to do some kind of exposé on psychics. "*Psychics are evil—next on John Walsh!*" And there I'd be, as an example of a fraud. I could actually understand the temptation of doing exposé shows like that. There are so many people out there who claim to be professional psychics and are really just out to scam people and make a quick buck that the whole psychic world is an easy target. I am not one of those people, but you never know what people are thinking.

As I entered the office building, I decided in my heart that right up front, I was going to be candid about what I could and could not do. It's one thing to be on *Good Morning Indiana* for 7 minutes and be forced to try and talk to the dead; it's quite another to have the producers of an internationally syndicated show waste their time with me. They would either like my approach or not—there was nothing I could do about that. But it was still hard not to be nervous. I was fairly positive that this meeting was a test to see what they could do with me. If I passed, they would put me on the air for much more than just a segment about jobs.

I felt the pressure as I sat in a boardroom, surrounded by about a dozen producers, and I moved from person to person, making eye contact with each one of them.

"Are you going to be able to look into the audience and see dead relatives and names?" one senior producer asked right away.

"That's not what I do," I said. I had resolved to be very honest about my strengths and weaknesses. "The only thing I can promise you is that if you let me come in with no expectations, there will be moments where you will be shocked. I can't guarantee what I will or won't see—you'll just have to let me do what I do," I summed up.

In television, that is asking a lot. In that moment in the boardroom, it was not me that I was trusting. It was God.

After our meeting, I got a call to set a date. They had decided to tape an hour-long show with me as the main guest. Topics of discussion would include "How to avoid a fake psychic" and "How can I become more psychic?"

Once the date was confirmed, I felt a 50-50 mix of excitement and utter terror. The longest television appearance I had ever made was maybe probably 12 min-

> So many people out there claim to be professional psychics and are really just out to scam people and make a quick buck. The whole psychic world is an easy target.

utes. This would be close to 38 minutes of all Dougall. That's a lot of time to be the main focus. If I thought about that any more, I would pass out, so I went on to a far more familiar and manageable neurosis: What on earth do I wear?

Now, you may think to yourself, *Did he meditate? Did he do a juice fast or sit in the lotus position to clear his channel? Chakra cleansing, something?* I opted for shopping therapy.

It's not just meditation that helps me prepare for my workday. Sometimes it's as simple as the outfit I wear. This is not about materialism; this is about feeling the best that I possibly can. Meditation and focus come naturally to me. Public speaking and presentation are things I have to work at.

"Do you think I should wear a suit on *John Walsh?*" was the question of the day.

I had about 2 weeks to decide. I asked everyone and their mother. David, my parents, Tarrin, the doorman. No matter how many times I told myself, *Don't ask too many people; it will just overwhelm you,* I could not stop myself from soliciting every last person's opinion.

My dad's suggestion was the best: a white dinner jacket and black pants. Sort of the cruise director look.

My goal was to look professional, to let people know that I take my work seriously. I did not want to look too corporate, so a suit was out, but in essence I was being given what felt like a great honor. I wanted Mr. Walsh to see that I respected him. I decided on black pinstriped pants and a black V-neck sweater with a white collared shirt underneath. You can never go wrong in black.

It's not uncommon for a talk show to tape and then never make it onto the air for whatever reason, so I decided that until I actually saw the listing in *TV Guide,* I would try not to tell too many more people about this. The time passed very quickly.

The night before I taped the show, I spent a very restless night. I tossed and turned, praying to be as relaxed as possible.

Dear God, tomorrow let me be a clear and wise channel. Please allow the perfect words to flow from my being. I ask that only those who I can assist be present in that room. Thank you for this opportunity to grow and learn from my own work as well as the lives of others. Oh, and if it's not too much trouble, some accurate readings would be great!

Rarely do I enter a work situation trying to be psychic, but I felt as though I needed an extra boost. For moral support, I had asked David to come to the studio with me. He could sit in the audience and see me in action. He was very excited, too—he wanted to support me personally, but it would also be his first time seeing what I did for a living.

"Do you really think you need coffee today?" David asked as we prepared to leave.

"I'm a basket case. Just humor me!"

There was no way I could actually drink that mug of java. I was sitting in the living room as David applied my makeup for the show. My heart was pounding like it was the first day of school.

"I'm almost done. You look adorable."

Now, you may think to yourself, *Did he meditate? Did he do a juice fast or sit in the lotus position to clear his channel?* Chakra cleansing? Nope. I opted for shopping therapy.

"Really?" I said.

"Really."

David kissed me and we went downstairs, where a car awaited us. This was a new perk for me. Every other show I had done didn't have nearly the budget to send a car for me. As the dark sedan pulled to a smooth stop in front of my building, I knew I was playing with the big boys.

We arrived at the NBC Studios about 2 hours before actual taping time. We were escorted into the building and taken to a dressing room. I had never had a dressing room before. It was pretty exciting, but nothing like you see in the movies. The room was furnished with a small gray love seat and a few chairs, nothing fancy. The best part was the silver tray resting on top of the small fridge. It was loaded with doughnuts and pastries.

"You've got to taste these doughnuts!" David mumbled, powdered sugar on his lips. He was happy.

"Are you insane? I am about to go on national television! All I want is a Tic Tac and a lemon wedge."

"Dougall, you look great. Here, I brought you a protein bar. *Eat it.*"

"I should probably meditate or something."

"Should I leave you alone?"

Knock-knock. . . . This was it!

Several producers came in. "Dougall, everyone is so excited for today," one of them started. "Let me explain how the show will work. We will start with John interviewing you about how you got started, for example."

The producer ran through every single question I would be asked. I understood what she was doing—making sure I wouldn't be caught off guard—but I prefer to hear and answer the questions in any interview live. There's no charge when the questions and answers are endlessly rehearsed. I'd heard the questions a million times before. I was finding it especially hard to generate enthusiasm with people coming in and out of the room every minute.

We finished the rundown of the show. Segment one: interview. Segment two: celebrity predictions. Segment three: reading for guests on stage. I was told that there would be people coming to find out about love, money, and career. That's it. No names. No descriptions. Nothing else (contrary to popular belief about psychics getting inside information off camera), all of which was perfect for me. Segment four: undercover camera. I had told the producers about some things gypsy psychics might say that were totally fake, and they had sent an undercover camera to see if that was true. Segment five: random readings for the audience.

Fifteen minutes before the show started, David was escorted to his seat. I was now alone. Alone with my thoughts.

Don't screw this up. You'll be fine. I want a doughnut. I wonder if John Walsh is nice. I should have worn a suit. I'm scared. I can't be scared. Be calm.

There was a tornado of thoughts in my mind. It was time for me to prepare for my work. I went back to the basics. I have used the same prayer before I work for years. I sat in the dressing room and closed my eyes.

I call upon the presence of all masters, teachers, angels, and guides. I allow myself to become a pure channel of love, light, and information. Allowing only that of the highest good to enter my being. As I unify in saying that I am of one mind and of one thought and of one vibration, and I ask that the mind be in me which is also in the christed consciousness.

The knock came, and I was ready.

John Walsh is probably one of the nicest people I have ever met.

He was gracious and interested as he welcomed me to the show, though I could tell he was a bit skeptical. He's a pretty hard-nosed, no-nonsense guy—a psychic probably wasn't his ideal choice for a guest. In fact, as the show opened, they had Mr. Walsh in the audience, asking how many people were believers and how many people were skeptics. He looked directly into the camera and stated that he was one of the skeptics. No pressure for me.

But as the hour went on, I could feel his mood changing. I even impressed myself when a woman stood up in the audience and I immediately saw the word "Boston" written in her aura. I came to find out she used to live there.

I spoke very candidly about how one could spot a fake psychic. I hear stories time and time again from people who are really being taken advantage of. There are psychics who in the middle of a session will tell you that for more money, they can see things more clearly. That is the dumbest thing I have ever heard in my life. Can you imagine if your medical doctor said that to you—"You know, for 50 more bucks, I could probably figure out what was wrong with you"? Come on!

Another common practice of fake psychics is to tell you that you either have a curse on you or suffer from bad luck. Lucky for you, they have a prayer system that you can buy, and they can instantly fix that. Quite frankly, this is a bunch of bullshit. So the *John Walsh* team decided to use a hidden camera on some of the street psychics in Manhattan to see if I was right. Sadly, each psychic used the same tricks of the trade that I had enumerated. They offered prayer to alleviate bad luck and spent the entire session trying to pry more money from their patrons. The lesson here applies to more than just psychics. Just about every industry has its quacks. There are fake doctors, lawyers, salespeople, and yes, even psychics.

Toward the end of my hour, I read for three audience members who came on-stage. Two of them were young women. I was not told anything about them except for the fact that they wanted to know about love. With the first woman, I was able to tell that she was in a relationship but was having problems.

As I looked at the next guest, I could only focus on one thing.

"Listen, I know I am supposed to talk about love, but I have to ask you. Have you ever acted before?"

"Yes, in high school."

"As soon as I look at you, all I want to talk about is being an actor. This is not a good time for relationships for you. I don't see a relationship until next summer. Someone with a name that starts with a B will come back into your life."

> There are psychics who, in the middle of a session, will tell you that for more money, they can see things more clearly. That is the dumbest thing I have ever heard in my life.

"It's so funny that you say that because I have been taking acting lessons lately, and I am not in a relationship right now."

John was clearly on my side by the time I finished with the third person, whom I told to look into journalism and to use his power with words in his career. He had been an English major in college and was now a writer and an actor. I was *on* that day. All in all, the show went phenomenally well—and the whole thing was over in what felt like only a few minutes. As I walked off the stage, my body was buzzing with energy. I was exhausted. I took a few pictures with Mr. Walsh, met some people offstage, and was taken back to the dressing

> Just about every industry has its quacks. There are fake doctors, lawyers, salespeople, and yes, even psychics.

room, where David was waiting for me. As I closed the door, I fell into his arms.

"You did so well! That was amazing. I am so proud of you!"

"Really?"

"Oh, my God, Dougall, I was so impressed."

In that moment, it was not about being on television and being seen by potentially millions of people. It was just another day of work, but it was the day that the person I loved got to see what I do. For me it was very special.

Knock-knock.

The producers came in and congratulated me on a wonderful job. They excitedly informed me that one of the "higher-ups" in charge of programming wanted to come down and meet me.

"Of course," I said, and the producers rushed back out as a group, leaving David and me to wait and see who was coming.

"What does this mean? What's going on?" David wondered.

"David, this is not that abnormal. I understand that it is a compliment. I must have made a good impression on someone, but don't get too excited."

Knock-knock.

A woman entered the dressing room. She had a warm smile and a firm handshake. She introduced herself as the executive in charge of finding new talent for NBC.

"Have you ever thought of having your own show?" she asked.

We talked for about 15 minutes, going through ideas for possible shows that I might be interested in doing. I must admit that for those 15 minutes, it felt great to be on the fun side of the television world. David looked shocked as we went back and forth about ratings, audiences, specials, and other psychic television shows we had seen. The executive was very straightforward and interested in what I had to say.

"It was really a pleasure to meet you. And I am really honored that you even came to talk to me about doing more work with NBC," I told her as she left. The moment she was gone, the producers came rushing back into the dressing room. My time was running out.

"Dougall, today was great! The car is waiting for you."

"Are you guys taping another show today?"

"We sure are."

"God, I'm exhausted. I can't imagine doing another show. Who is it with?"

"Oh, Chaka Kahn's our next guest."

As I stood up from my chair, I took a deep breath. I was sharing a dressing room with the likes of Chaka Khan! There was no other way to say it: That was cool.

About 3 days later, I was informed that my episode of *The John Walsh Show* would air in about 10 days.

"Let's have a viewing party!" David said.

"That's a great idea."

It was a special occasion on so many fronts. My mother had never seen me live on TV. Over the years, I had sent her tapes of other appearances, but to watch a show live is much more exciting.

The show aired in New York at 12 noon. That morning, I woke up at about 9:45. Like every other day, I signed on to check my e-mail.

"You've got mail!"

I gazed at the screen and scrolled down to click on my e-mails. It was taking a long time.

"Holy shit, I have over 300 e-mails!" I cried out to David, and he came running over to look. I couldn't believe it, but we didn't have time to read. I had a party to get ready for.

By the end of the day, I had received over 2,000 e-mails.

> Dear Dougall, I have just watched you on *The John Walsh Show*. You are amazing—you have a new fan in Arizona!

> Dear Dougall, I just watched you on *The John Walsh Show*. You are so funny. I really enjoyed it and felt very touched by what you said.

Ninety percent of the e-mails were wonderful. People were very nice to drop me a note and tell me how much they enjoyed the show. By the end of the weekend, I had thousands of e-mails. I was determined to respond to each of them. But some of them were very difficult.

> Dear Dougall, I have stage-four lymphoma. Ever since watching you on The John Walsh Show, I feel as if you are the only person who can help me.

> Dear Dougall, My daughter was kidnapped about a year ago. Please tell us where she is.

> Dear Dougall, You are a horrible person. I think you are the devil, and shame on you for taking advantage of people. You are doing the devil's work.

I answered close to 1,000 of them, plugging away night after night until David finally came in to get me in the very early hours of the morning. I was so absorbed, I didn't even hear him coming until I felt his hand on my shoulder.

"Dougall, you can't possibly answer all of these people."

"I know, but they all took the time to write me a note, and some of them are really nice."

"Yeah, but you obsess so much about the sad ones."

It's true; they were all I could talk about. Some of them were long, detailed e-mails from women who were being beaten by their husbands. Kids who were lonely and needed a friend. Questions on how to become more psychic.

My e-mail account became reminiscent of the psychic line. But on the psychic line, I had been more than once removed from the callers. This flood of e-mails was directed right at me. I had to face the fact: There is only so much I can do.

Chapter Sixteen

THIS IS WHAT I KNOW

I GOT ON THE SUBWAY THE OTHER DAY TO HEAD OFF TO THE OFFICE AS USUAL. I had a little extra spring in my step because I knew that in exactly 2 weeks, I would be leaving to go on vacation. I had my coffee in one hand and a copy of the *New York Daily News* in the other, just another workday morning.

The train screeched into place at Forty-second Street, and a woman entered my car.

"Oh, no," I said out loud, knowing what was coming.

"Ladies and gentlemen, I have an announcement from the FBI," she announced matter-of-factly to the car at large.

This woman is familiar to me and probably many other subway riders in my area. She is not what you'd expect from your average crazy New Yorker. She looks to be in her mid-to-late thirties, and she's an attractive, well-groomed African American woman. On this day, she was wearing a sundress with a T-shirt underneath. If I passed her on the street, I wouldn't give her a second glance. To the outside world, she appeared quite normal, until she started talking.

"Ladies and gentleman, I have spoken with Agent Charles of the FBI, and he is tired—I repeat, *tired*—of the Jehovah's Witnesses." She looked around to make sure we had all gotten the message. Then she continued.

"Ladies and gentlemen, the FBI is working undercover with the Jehovah's Witnesses, and they are tired. Just the other day, I was at a meeting with the Asian Jehovah's Witnesses, and agents Charles and Dunn asked me to give you this message."

She looked at each person on the subway with great intent. She had a serious look on her face, as if it were her solemn duty to relay this message to morning commuters. I had seen her just 2 weeks ago—same train, same stop, similar message.

"Ladies and gentlemen, if you receive an Airborne Express package, just ignore it!"

I made eye contact with the woman across from me. We both started to laugh quietly.

There is somewhat of an unspoken rule on the New York subway. It is against protocol for strangers to actually speak to one another; you have to communicate with your eyes only. At that moment, the stranger across from me and I were silently discussing the lunatic on our car.

Our FBI contact continued to fill us in on the drama surrounding a certain religious community and the FBI in a loud voice as my coconspirator and I held back smiles. The car stopped at Thirty-fourth Street, and our undercover agent left us to spread her message further.

"You *will* hear from me again," she promised as she stepped off the train.

Five or six of us passengers darted glances back and forth at one another. Then I did something rare: I spoke aloud.

"I've seen her before."

"Really? She looks so normal," the woman sitting next to me answered.

"What the hell was she talking about?" my giggle partner across the way asked.

"Oh, this was nothing today—usually she gets much angrier," I informed them. For the next three stops, we talked about the little intrusion on our commute and crazy people on public transportation in general. It was just another New York moment—never, ever dull.

I got off at my stop, Twenty-third Street, and walked down the busy street toward my office, musing about all the different kinds of people in the world. It's only been 5 years, so I don't know if I am a real New Yorker yet, but I feel like I've seen it all—and a lot of it at very close range. On any given workday, I delve deeply into the personal lives of many others. I speak to people all across the world, doing my best to be present but, more importantly, urging people to take control of their lives. I want them to realize that the information that they are looking for, the answer they are hoping to find, can't come from one session with me.

When I arrived at my office, my first session was over the phone, with a new female client named Pat. When I heard her voice, I immediately sensed that she had major body issues. I knew that she was paranoid about her body and criticized it constantly.

I always want to be authentic, yes—but cruel, no. I would never start a session with anything that could be construed negatively; I always try to ease into problem areas gently. So I opened with, "I

> On any given workday, I delve deeply into the personal lives of many others. I do my best to be present, but more importantly, I urge people to take control of their lives.

feel you have perfection issues. You criticize yourself constantly—you need to stop that!" I laughed a little at my own chiding tone so it wouldn't sound too harsh.

"It is my feeling that, as a child, your boundaries were overrun and your space was invaded." I waited for a response, to see if she was ready to talk about this. Silence; so I continued. "The image I'm seeing in my head is when I was sexually abused as a child." I often use my own experience in this way because I want clients to identify with me and feel comfortable speaking about anything with me.

Still nothing, so I probed a little. "Does that make sense? Because I'm feeling that you were sexually abused, though I could be wrong." Again, I was feeling my way gently—I didn't say straight out, "You were sexually abused," though I know this was the case.

Pat started crying and said, "Yes, I was."

From her energy so far, I surmised that this woman hadn't worked for a year. "I see you haven't worked for a year," I went on.

Well, I thought it had been a year. She told me, "Actually, I haven't worked for 10 years."

"I also feel that you are agoraphobic. I feel afraid of the world when I talk to you." I could sense she didn't have any friends and never went out of her house, to work, socialize, or do anything else.

"Pat, money is tight," I continued. "You really can't afford me." We kept talking, and it turned out that Pat had no money, no job, and no social life and had maxed out all her credit cards. She had an alcoholic father and had indeed been sexually abused. Pat was calling me because she wanted me to tell her that a new job was right around the corner—one in which she wouldn't have to leave her house. That a relationship was going to come knocking on the door, literally. She wanted to hear that her life was going to change and that she would feel great the minute she got off the phone with me. And that's just not true.

The first thing I tried was to get Pat to open up to the idea of therapy. "I don't have the tools or the education to help you through these serious issues left over from childhood. But you need a safe place with someone who you feel free to talk to."

She quickly cut me off. "I hate therapy."

"Look, I go to therapy, and I don't necessarily like it, but it's important that I go."

"I can't afford it."

Now I was getting a little frustrated. "You certainly had the courage to find the money to pay for me, and the truth is, I'm probably a lot more expensive than a therapist in your area. There are college campuses where students who are studying psychology will see you for free. There are support groups for incest survivors." I went through a whole litany of suggestions. We were now 20 minutes into the session, and neither one of us was pleased. Every time I presented something, she shut it down. Finally I said, "Pat, this is your reading. So why don't you ask me any questions you have, and I'll do my best to answer them."

"Am I going to get married?"

"I'm sorry, Pat. You are not. Not everything is written in stone, but right now I'm reading your energy. You spend every minute in your home. The universe will not drop a husband off at your doorstep."

"Am I going to get a job?"

"Pat, you could certainly work. Because of your physical disabilities, at the moment we need to first work on these limitations that are keeping you from getting a job."

She was really mad. "This is so disappointing. This is just throwing away money. I can't believe I called you. You haven't really told me anything!"

"Pat, you are paying me to see things about you." I wasn't literally seeing her, of course, as this session was over the phone, but I could sense everything I needed to know in her voice. I had done my job, and a pretty good, accurate job at that.

"Let me give you some final words of advice. Like every person on this earth, you were born with an outline for your life, a template. What you do with that outline is up to you. You have a physical disability that renders you unable to leave the house. How you handle that condition is up to you.

"I've given you some ideas. There are places that work with people who have disabilities, and they will place you in a job. I don't care if you work for an hour a month and make 10 cents. I guarantee you will feel better.

"Pat, do me a favor. For 6 months, try to shift your thoughts. You can laugh at me in your head. You can think, *Dougall is a jackass, and nothing he says will work.* But if you really commit to changing the way you think and try to become more open to some of these new ideas I mentioned, and you call me 6 months from now and nothing has changed, I will give you your money back for this session."

> Like every person on this earth, you were born with an outline for your life, a template. What you do with that outline is up to you.

"This has been a complete waste of my time."

"I'm sorry you feel that way. All I can tell you is that until you shift your thoughts, you will stay in misery. It's up to you."

Now, you have to remember that this woman had been waiting 5 months for her reading, and she was very excited. She had saved her money and been greatly anticipating being on the phone with someone she saw on TV. To Pat, I'm a celebrity. She saw the fun part on TV—the audience, the lights, the amazing things I pulled out of the air. But I'm not a genius. I can't change people's lives overnight. She wanted me to fix everything for her, and I couldn't.

Predictions are easy for me and fun. But do people *listen* to me? Very few. Even in the psychic world, there are no quick fixes.

I pride myself on my ability to connect with people on an emotional level in my work. I understand your concerns; I can feel your fears. My career has evolved to the point where I feel comfortable doing some life coaching in my readings, as I tried to do with Pat. I've learned that most people would prefer that I read their minds and tell them what to do. Most people just want the answers so they can sit back. The thing most people want, I've discovered, is a driver.

But I can only *see and point out* these things! From that moment on, it's up to you to change things for yourself. I would estimate that about 20 percent of the people I read for actually listen to what I say and take steps to change their lives. Predictions are easy for me and fun. People tell me constantly, "You were right on the money." But do people *listen* to me? Very few.

I have had to accept the idea that many people like Pat come to a psychic because it's their last resort, and they're looking for a quick fix. But even in the psychic world, there are no quick fixes. When I hang up with a caller like Pat, I feel just awful. It would be so easy for me to say exactly what they want to hear. And sure, in that moment, I would feel good because she would be happy, she would effusively thank me and think I was great, and Pat would get her hopes up and spirits briefly lifted. But in 3 years, when nothing I said happens and this person's life is still the exact same, where does that leave both of us?

So I tell the truth. But now there's a woman out there who thinks what I did was crap and she wasted her money. In my heart, do I know that I did my job properly? Absolutely. If I can't connect with you within the first 10 minutes, I cut the session short and you don't get charged. I know when I've done my job and when I haven't. With Pat, I more than did my job; she just didn't like the outcome.

That is another downside of working as a psychic: People are not always prepared for what they will hear. Everybody thinks it's such a great idea to hire me for private parties. "Oh, it's going to be so much fun! We'll get our futures told!" Though I did eventually break my own rule and do a few private functions after my last horrible event in Dallas, to this day I turn down 99 percent of party requests. There's just not enough money to put up with the aggravation.

I made an exception recently for a friend of mine who has her own business. She has a stable of experts from various fields, and women's groups book them as special guest speakers at their functions. For example, once a group went to Barney's, and my friend's personal shopper joined them to teach them all what to wear, their best colors and styles, and then they all went off to have lunch. Things like that— it's all very light and fun.

So when my friend asked me if I would do one of her parties, I agreed. Twenty women had gathered in Manhattan, in one of the biggest apartments I had ever been inside of. I got paid a very nice amount of money to do a quick spiel and a brief reading for each woman. In the middle of the party, one of the women left. She went up to the hostess and said, "He's amazing, but I don't even want him to look at me," then walked out the door. I'm guessing it was because I was coming up with things like "Your husband hasn't touched you in 4 years." It was pretty heavy.

Yes, the women were all friends, but not quite good enough friends to talk about things like that. "Do you want to talk about his drinking problem?" Stuff like that was just rolling out of me—I was dead-on. And the room was dead silent.

This kind of thing tends to be a problem. People think a psychic reading is going to be all fun and light and nice. They think they'll hear little fortune-cookie sayings or harmless little things like "Your husband's name is Rob," so they

That is another downside of working as a psychic: People are not always prepared for what they will hear.

can squeal and run away and giggle with their friends and down a few more Cosmos. And that's not the way it works. Sure, I can do little party tricks. It's very easy and fun for me. But there are times when the floodgates open and I have to say what I feel.

My friend pulled me aside for a little conference after the party was over. "Dougall, don't get me wrong—that was wonderful. You were amazing, and I'd love to have you do more events. But next time, we've got to set it up differently. Someone walked out of the party! Those women were totally freaked-out!"

"I know. I warned you it would happen!" No one ever listens. But I agreed to do one more event for my friend, which we handled differently. After I did my spiel, I brought out a hat so everyone could drop their names in. At that point, several women opted out. They

People think psychic readings are all fun and light. That they'll hear little fortune cookie sayings or harmless things like "Your husband's name is Rob," so they can squeal and giggle with their friends and down a few more Cosmos. And that's not the way it works.

said, "I've heard enough; I don't want my name in the hat." Then I did private readings in the other room, out of everyone's earshot.

I am fine with people who don't want to be read for. I understand them, even more so than people who are dying to get a reading. I respect them for knowing that they have issues they are not ready to face head-on and deal with. It's a kick to have someone look at you and tell you things about yourself. But sometimes there are things you are not quite ready to hear, and I am fine with people who don't want to know.

There are certain readings I call the whip-you-into-shape readings. These are not fun to give or get. I've gotten e-mail from clients who tell me, "I don't think I would ever like to have another reading again in my life." The energy I feel coming through my body at these times is very different. It's dense and direct. When I reach you and get to the heart of the issue, I have to come out with it. There are many people who leave my office stunned. I always tell clients who call my office to book an appointment that they should write their questions down. Because I will speak to you for 15 minutes straight before you get the chance to speak. Nine times out of 10, after my 15 minutes, when I ask if they have any questions, all I hear is complete silence. Then they say, "I have no idea what to say right now." Because I've gone bang-bang-bang right through their life, and they are completely freaked-out by it.

I certainly try to take a client's personality into account. Some people are stronger and more self-aware than others. Some people will laugh and shake their head and say, "Yes, that's me. . . . You found me out." They're all right with it, and we laugh and have fun. They're more direct. They're the kind of person who'll say something like, "Yeah, I know this guy is a loser, but the sex is damn good."

"But you can do that on your own," I point out. Then we laugh even more. It's good to have clients who have some awareness of their own stuff. It's the ones who have it so deeply buried that they haven't even consciously faced it who tend to be unpleasantly surprised during a reading.

Another downside to my job: the people who dismiss my abilities out of hand. No matter what I do—make astonishing predictions that come true or give someone the most insightful reading they could ever hope for, plenty of people just don't buy what I'm all about. And I think that's because they don't understand it. Everyone has psychic intuition. Everyone gets cues and clues from the universe. I am just more tuned in to them.

I think most people will agree that psychic impressions can manifest as a sense of danger. Nobody questions a mom who says she knows that something bad has happened to her child. Fear is the easiest psychic reaction to pick up because the body creates an actual chemical, physical reaction in response to being threatened. There are hundreds of stories where people felt a sense of danger and didn't get on that plane that went down. Or knew that a fire was coming and evacuated the house. All kinds of stories.

An extreme example of this phenomenon is a woman walking alone at night who sees a man across the street and gets an immediate feeling of danger. Many times a woman in this situation does nothing and winds up getting raped or assaulted. Sadly, I have heard this story more than a few times. I have sat across from women, with tears streaming down their faces after reliving their attacks, who tell me, "I knew something was wrong when I saw him, but I just felt like I was being judgmental!" They have certainly paid a heavy price for ignoring their own intuition.

Let's take the polar opposite of Pat for a moment. My friend Nancy is an extremely successful television producer. Smart, together, happily married, successful. She and her husband had been trying for a long time to adopt a baby, and after many searches, she connected with a birth mother in a faraway state. She called me all excited. "We've found the perfect birth mother in New Mexico! It will be a private adoption. We're putting her in an apartment and paying her rent, bought her a car. She's about 4 months along, and we could not be more excited. . . . We're flying out to meet her next month. . . . Isn't this the most wonderful thing?"

When Nancy and her husband arrived in New Mexico, they learned that the woman had stolen the car, had never been pregnant, and was pulling this scam on several other couples at the same time. My friend had great connections and immediately got herself on the local televi-

> **Most people agree that psychic impressions can manifest as a sense of danger. Nobody questions a mom who says she knows that something bad has happened to her child.**

sion station, telling her story and saying directly to the camera, "I will find you." The woman was found and arrested, but the whole ordeal took Nancy down. She's an extremely strong woman and tough, but this really threw her for a loop. She was desperately sad and couldn't forgive herself for having been scammed like that. We were on the phone one night when she said for the 10th time, "I just can't believe I didn't notice anything wrong."

"I want you to do me a favor, Nancy. Take a deep breath, relax, breathe. Focus on the very first time you made contact with this woman. How did that go? When is the first time you saw her or spoke to her?"

"Well, we e-mailed back and forth; then she sent me a picture," Nancy said.

"Think back for a minute here. When you opened the envelope and pulled out her picture, what was the very first thought that went through your mind?"

Nancy was quiet for a moment, then said, "I thought it looked like a mug shot."

"So your heart didn't tell you, *Criminal, thief, this woman will steal from me and break my heart*. But it said, *Mug shot*. This is how I interpret *mug shot*: criminal behavior, something's not right. What was your second thought?"

"I told myself, *You are being a rich, spoiled bitch and extremely judgmental.*"

"Your soul gave you a message, and you ignored it. It's not the end of the world, but just an example of intuition and listening to your heart."

The ability is there for everyone; I am just highly skilled at picking up and interpreting the energy and impressions we all receive. That's really all being "psychic" means, so why is it that no one wants to accept the fact that I can predict the outcome of a love relationship, but they have no problem believing that a mom "knows" something is wrong with one of their kids? It's the same thing; I'm just channeling it in a different direction!

I *am* a channel. When I am sitting with you, the universe is speaking through me. Quite honestly, I don't think it's going to make a big difference in your life if we talk about whether or not your boyfriend is coming back for the rest of your life. Yes, doing just that is a big part of what keeps me in business. But that is not what I *truly* do. The fact is, the universe doesn't really care about whether or not your boyfriend is coming back. What the universe cares about is *why* you want your boyfriend back.

There are many women (and men) out there—I see them every day—who are not really functioning at their peak when they're on their own. This is why relationship issues are such a big part of my business. Everybody wants to know when they're going to find someone. What I try to tell unattached clients is this: If you're single and not involved in a sexual relationship with someone, I don't care about that. What I want to do is make sure you are taking care of yourself as a whole, unified being. That you've got a job, you're paying your rent, you're getting dressed every day, socializing, exercising—and that you're having sex, even though you don't have anyone in your life. If no one special is in your life, you should be having sex with yourself! People, the word is masturbation. (When

> **The universe doesn't really care about whether or not your boyfriend is coming back. What the universe cares about is *why* you want your boyfriend back.**

I'm reading for a shy woman in a small town in Wisconsin and I bring this up, she's shocked. "What did you say!?")

I'm sorry, but come on. Quit bitching that you don't have a relationship—live the life you want to live. Go to the movies, take yourself out to dinner, go out for a cup of coffee, buy yourself flowers. Everything that you would do if you were in a relationship, make sure it's all still part of your life. That way you're not focused on what's missing.

Everybody's looking at "the lack." "I don't have a boyfriend." "I don't have a husband." "I'm not having sex." "My girlfriend dumped me." Trust me; it's not only single people who have sexual problems. When I'm reading for a client in a relationship, I tap into his or her heart. I don't know how to put into words the way that I do that, but I do a quick check to see if their heart is satisfied. Then I check into their physical structure to see if they are physically satisfied. I'm always amazed at how many people in relationships aren't. And this is not something they talk about or bring up.

What I'm trying to do is get my clients to find what will make their lives the most satisfying and fulfilling. I want them to feel whole, with partners or without. Let's face it: Desperation is such a turnoff. When you're on a date and the other person senses that you are trying too hard to make something happen because you want a relationship so badly, they usually don't ever call again. Desperation and longing do not thrive in the universe. Satisfaction and satiety, which require taking care of yourself, do.

Living a successful life is all about understanding and working with the laws of attraction. This applies to the business world as well as to the romantic sphere. When I'm interviewing someone for a job and they are too eager to be hired, it's a turnoff. After many hard lessons, I've now learned that when I'm approached by producers, I won't dress like a gypsy or change my name to Sir Dougall or whatever silly thing they may propose that doesn't honor who I am. If we have a common vision, if I can do my job and help people and have fun—and maybe even make a difference—well, then, I'm all for it. But other than that, I'm not interested. I'm happy where I am, and that's enough.

When you are living the laws of attraction, what you want comes to you much more easily. I have done, and continue to do, my best to follow my own advice. I myself have not had a psychic reading for many years, and I think that's because I am finally content. I live my life by my own rules and strive to live up to my own standards. Sure, occasionally I read my horoscope for entertainment purposes. When I go into a bookstore, I always check out the aisle with the tarot cards and other New Age toys. C'mon—who can resist? But after many years of being obsessed with getting readings and all the latest gadgets, they are just a hobby now. I don't get any psychic readings, but I now give them on a daily basis. The demand is there and remains steady. My re-peat business is at an all-time high. Why is that?

To be completely honest, I believe that the main reason people come for a psychic reading is that they're in pain. Say you've lost your job, or your partner abandoned you for someone else, or your child is seriously ill—there's a part of people that naturally wonders, *If there really is a God, why am I suffering like this?*

Ultimately, my goal really *isn't* to give reading after reading, making people dependent on me or my guidance. Instead, my goal is to show you that you have the answers. What makes a psychic reading so intense is that I show people that I can pick up on these things, these painful issues, without their saying a word. I can also teach them to see energy that's all around us, every second. But you don't need my help to figure out your own direction in life—I am only a kick start. It's what you do *after* your reading, not what is said *during* one, that is where your true destiny lies.

When we start to understand these laws of the universe, we start to realize that there's actually a reason why each and every one of us is on this planet. It's not some cosmic fluke; we all go through our own trials for a reason. There is a higher power leading us to something, whatever that may be. For me personally, there's a great sense of safety in that. I genuinely believe that everything has a reason.

That is the bottom line of my readings: What is your reason for being on this planet? It is my heartfelt desire to steer you toward living your best life, the one you were meant to have.

From the time I was a kid, all I wanted was to be a psychic because I thought it was the epitome of spiritual advancement. I now know that being psychic and being spiritually evolved are two very different things because, for a long time, I was a pretty good psychic with a pretty screwed-up life. I strive every day to become more spiritually evolved, kinder, more loving and tolerant—in short, a better person in every way. As for work, I no longer enter a session trying to tell the future. Instead, I enter a session trying to see my clients the way that God created them. And "God" is just a term . . . Buddha, Running Eagle, higher power, Muhammed, the Universe—whatever you want to call it. It's all the same thing: an eternal source of love. That's all any of us, I believe, are looking for, a place where we are in a state of grace. And when I'm giving you a reading, my job is to see you the way the universe sees you: perfect.

It's what you do *after* your reading, not what is said *during* one, that is where your true destiny lies.